Statistics in psychology

Statistics in psychology

Explanations without equations

Stephen Jones

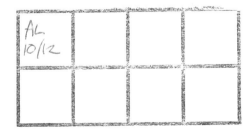

palgrave
macmillan

First published 2010 by
PALGRAVE MACMILLAN

Palgrave Macmillan in the UK is an imprint of Macmillan Publishers Limited, registered in England, company number 785998, of Houndmills, Basingstoke, Hampshire RG21 6XS.

Palgrave Macmillan in the US is a division of St Martin's Press LLC, 175 Fifth Avenue, New York, NY 10010.

Palgrave Macmillan is the global academic imprint of the above companies and has companies and representatives throughout the world.

Palgrave® and Macmillan® are registered trademarks in the United States, the United Kingdom, Europe and other countries.

ISBN: 978–0–230–24749–9

This book is printed on paper suitable for recycling and made from fully managed and sustained forest sources. Logging, pulping and manufacturing processes are expected to conform to the environmental regulations of the country of origin.

A catalogue record for this book is available from the British Library.

A catalog record for this book is available from the Library of Congress.

10 9 8 7 6 5 4 3 2 1
19 18 17 16 15 14 13 12 11 10

Printed in China

To Dawn and Ray –
for the buttonholes and the bouquets

Contents

List of illustrations   x
Preface   xiii
Acknowledgements   xvi

chapter 1 **Variables and participants**   **1**
  1.1 Variables and their measurement   3
     1.1.1 Concepts   3
     1.1.2 Everyday examples   5
     1.1.3 From the literature   8
     1.1.4 Narrative   18
     1.1.5 Further reading   21
  1.2 Research design   23
     1.2.1 Concepts   23
     1.2.2 Everyday examples   25
     1.2.3 From the literature   27
     1.2.4 Narrative   30
     1.2.5 Further reading   34
  1.3 Summary   35
  Chapter 1 self-test   37

chapter 2 **Descriptive statistics**   **39**
  2.1 Summarizing findings via measures of
     central tendency   41
     2.1.1 Concepts (Mode, Median and Mean)   41
     2.1.2 Everyday examples   43
     2.1.3 From the literature   47
     2.1.4 Narrative   50
     2.1.5 Further reading   51
  2.2 Summarizing findings via measures
     of dispersion   52
     2.2.1 Concepts (Range and Interquartile
         range, Variance, Standard deviation)   52
     2.2.2 Everyday examples   54
     2.2.3 From the literature   56

	2.2.4	Narrative	59
	2.2.5	Further reading	61
2.3	Summarizing findings via percentiles and standard scores		62
	2.3.1	Concepts (Percentiles and Z-scores)	62
	2.3.2	Everyday examples	63
	2.3.3	From the literature	67
	2.3.4	Narrative	69
	2.3.5	Further reading	71
2.4	Summary		72
	Chapter 2 self-test		74

chapter 3 Prelude to testing — **76**

3.1	Populations, samples and standard errors		78
	3.1.1	Concepts	78
	3.1.2	Examples and illustrations	81
	3.1.3	Further reading	84
3.2	Hypothesis testing, probability and the statistical significance		85
	3.2.1	Concepts	85
	3.2.2	Examples and illustrations	87
	3.2.3	Further reading	91
3.3	Parametric assumptions		92
	3.3.1	Concepts	92
	3.3.2	Examples and illustrations	95
	3.3.3	Further reading	99
	3.3.4	Narrative	100
3.5	Summary		103
	Chapter 3 self-test		105

chapter 4 Inferential statistics — **107**

4.1	Parametric testing		110
	4.1.1	Concepts (Difference between, Difference within, Correlation)	110
	4.1.2	Everyday examples	112
	4.1.3	From the literature	120
	4.1.4	Narrative	135
	4.1.5	Further reading	141
4.2	Non-parametric testing (ordinal)		142
	4.2.1	Concepts (Difference between, Difference within, Correlation)	142
	4.2.2	Everyday examples	144
	4.2.3	From the literature	150
	4.2.4	Narrative	165

	4.2.5	Further reading	170
4.3	Non-parametric testing (nominal)		171
	4.3.1	Concepts (Difference between, Difference within)	171
	4.3.2	Everyday examples	172
	4.3.3	From the literature	177
	4.3.4	Narrative	190
	4.3.5	Further reading	193
4.4	Summary		194
Chapter 4 self-test			195

And finally... 198

Appendix	200
Glossary	202
References	210
Answers to self-tests	215
Index	219

Illustrations

Tables

1.1 Illustrative studies in terms of their main
methodological features   16

1.2 Aspects of the reaction time study in terms of types
of variables and levels of measurement   21

1.3 Illustrative studies in terms of their main
methodological features   29

1.4 Aspects of the reaction time study in terms of research
design and levels of measurement   33

2.1 Standard deviations of self-estimates on five ability
scales. Adapted from Rammstedt and Rammsayer (2000)   57

2.2 Aspects of the reaction time study in terms of
research design and levels of measurement   60

2.3 Addition of Z-scores on individual variables into
an 'alertness index'   70

3.1 Comparison between concepts based on means,
and concepts based on *mean* of means   80

3.2 Examples of null, experimental, directional hypotheses   89

3.3 Summary table of Type I and Type II errors   90

3.4 Results of tests for normality (via skew and kurtosis)
and equal variances (via Levene)   97

3.5 Aspects of the reaction time study including sampling
and suitability for parametric testing   100

3.6 Standard error figures for the clubbing and
non-clubbing samples   101

3.7 Skew and kurtosis figures for the clubbing and
non-clubbing samples   101

3.8 Use of the Levene statistic to check for comparable
variances   101

4.1   Organization and structure of Chapter 4   109
4.2   Means, skew and kurtosis of the two samples   113
4.3   Results of the Levene and the independent t-test   114
4.4   Means and SDs of the two conditions   116
4.5   Skew and kurtosis of the differences   116
4.6   Results of the paired t-test   117
4.7   Skew and kurtosis results of the two variables   118
4.8   Results of the Pearson correlation coefficient   119
4.9   Means, skew and kurtosis of the two samples   136
4.10   Results of the Levene and the independent t-test   137
4.11   Skew and kurtosis of the differences   138
4.12   Results of the paired t-test   138
4.13   Skew and kurtosis results of the two variables   139
4.14   Results of the Pearson correlation coefficient   140
4.15   Mann-Whitney ranks   145
4.16   Mann-Whitney statistics   145
4.17   Wilcoxon ranks   147
4.18   Wilcoxon test statistics   147
4.19   Results of the Spearman correlation coefficient   149
4.20   Mann-Whitney ranks   166
4.21   Mann-Whitney statistics   166
4.22   Wilcoxon ranks   167
4.23   Wilcoxon statistics   167
4.24   Results of the Spearman correlation coefficient   170
4.25   Sample 2 × 2 chi square grids   173
4.26   Cross-tabs of belief in Santa by age   174
4.27   Chi square statistic for belief in Santa by age   174
4.28   Cross-tabs of voting intention before PPB by after PPB   177
4.29   Statistics of voting intention before PPB by after PPB   177
4.30   The number of trials where help was offered before
       and after 70 seconds   179
4.31   Participant behaviour following receipt of mobile ads   181
4.32   Cross-tabs of Sex × Drinking, Sex × Eating and
       Eating × Drinking   184
4.33   Cross-tabs of pre- and post-intervention decisions
       regarding disciplinary actions   189
4.34   Cross-tabs of completion by Thursday night activities   191
4.35   Chi square statistics of completion by Thursday
       night activities   191

4.36 Cross-tabs of task completion before lunch by after lunch   193
4.37 Statistics of task completion before lunch by after lunch   193

Figures

2.1 Relationship between percentiles, Z-scores and T-scores   66
3.1 Spread of sample means approximating to a
     normal distribution   83
3.2 Distribtion of IQ scores at Uni. A   96
3.3 Distribution of IQ scores at Uni. B   96
4.1 Scatter plot of hours watching TV by test results   120
4.2 Scatter plot of the relationship between reaction time
     and 'party time'   140
4.3 Scatter plot of the relationship between test ranking
     and book ratings   149
4.4 Scatter plot of the relationship between experiment
     ratings and ranked position   169

Preface

This book has come into being largely as a result of the requests of hundreds (nay, thousands) of psychology students being taught on a research methods and statistics module over many years – far more years than I would care to remember. Actually, that's not quite true – it's perhaps more because of hundreds (nay, thousands) of questions such as 'why do we have to do this stuff?' and comments such as 'but I really just don't get numbers!' that this book has found its way into your hands.

There are various responses applicable to the 'why do we do this?' question, including reassurances that studying statistics in psychology will help us to understand the discipline more effectively (almost from a sort of 'understanding from within' viewpoint); that it will help us think more critically (you'll certainly be less likely to simply accept on face value the 'facts and figures' you'll see reported in the media after reading this book); and of course that it's essential for the BPS accreditation process (which is usually the clincher!).

Another response to this question is that it can actually be enjoyable! You may have some initial difficulty with that last reason at the moment, but think about it for a moment – you're doing a psychology degree (at least I would assume this is the case if you're reading this book?) and presumably you are doing this degree because you're interested in its subject matter. Now where did this subject matter come from? How did all that stuff in your other text books actually get there? Well, unless some radical transformation within the discipline of psychology has taken place between the time this script was sent to the publishers and the time it hit the bookshelves, it's pretty certain that everything in the other textbooks was derived from the findings of research. So, how did these findings come about? (I think you may be able to see where I'm going with this ...?). Well, they were derived via numerous research processes, many of which incorporated this mysterious phenomenon of statistics. Now, assuming that we are interested in psychology, it should not be too great a leap to develop an interest in how the discipline itself has come to be – of how the knowledge contained in your other textbooks - be this on child rearing, ability testing, memory facility, personality factors, behavioural disorders or the physiology of the nervous system – has been produced?

This represents the first aim of this book – to help you understand the principles of quantitative research and to understand when certain research procedures should and should not be used in the production of 'psychological knowledge'. In this sense it is very similar to most of the other books on research methods and data analysis currently available. Where this one differs is in how it tries to achieve this, that is, via reference to everyday examples and actual psychological studies. It therefore tries to emphasize the psychological, rather than the statistical, by focusing on the situations where we may encounter statistics on a day-to-day basis almost without realizing it, and also by emphasizing the contribution which statistics has made to a series of studies drawn from the psychological literature – these studies reflecting the breadth of the discipline, ranging from investigations into eating disorders and problem drinking, the use of mobile phones and social networking sites, to the brain physiology of taxi drivers and the shared sense of humour of sexual partners. The book has therefore adopted a 'learning by example' approach whenever possible, which will hopefully reinforce the notion that statistics is used very much as a tool within psychology – a method by which we investigate our research question – rather than as an end in itself.

The second aim of this book is to deal with the 'I just don't get numbers' type of comment, which is perhaps an understandable situation considering the diversity of the discipline and the varied backgrounds of its students. Psychology attracts entrants from those with backgrounds in a wide variety of subject areas, many of which are arts and humanities based, and where students have not engaged with many aspects of numeracy for perhaps several years. Many are therefore surprised to find upon enrolment that their BPS accredited course requires coverage of a substantial statistical element, and that this can account for over 20% of a student's modular content just during year one. Even those entering with the psychology A-Level are frequently surprised by the statistical content of the degree programme, as the subject is treated quite differently on degree programmes from the way with which it is dealt at A-Level (see Conway and Bannister 2007). This book therefore aims to address these issues by avoiding numbers wherever possible. Statistical concepts will be explained via examples, analogies and scenarios – both hypothetical and real – rather than by referring to any formulae or calculations. There are plenty of other texts which enable those who may be interested to see how the statistics we use are actually derived and how we can perform step-by-step calculations to obtain our results – indeed reference will be made to such texts throughout the book – but the bottom line is that this book just isn't going to go there!

So if you are one of those students who were more than a little surprised to find so much statistical content on your degree, or weren't a particularly big fan of GCSE maths, or just don't find the prospect of reading through pages and pages of numbers and weird little symbols particularly appealing, then this could be just the thing to help guide you along the path of quantitative data analysis … :-).

Acknowledgements

I'd like to thank Věrka, David and Laura for their patience in listening to me babbling on about some of these offbeat ideas, and to Jamie Joseph and the team at Palgrave Macmillan for allowing me to convert them into a real-life tangible item. Also, thanks to all who've worked with me on RDM/RDA over the years, and to all at the Prague Thursdays – particularly Ise for that initial conversation in Velryba. Finally, I should express my appreciation to the several thousand students I've taught over the last ten years, whose general confusion and occasional fear when confronted with symbols and numbers gave me the idea that a book like this might not be such a bad idea....

All SPSS screenshots are taken from SPSS Statistics 17, Rel. 17.0.0. 2008. Chicago: SPSS Inc.

Almost all research in Psychology – and thus the collection and analysis of psychological data – is based on the concept of variables. A variable in the simplest sense is something that can change; in other words, something that varies! It is a factor, characteristic or feature which can vary over time, or between situations or between people. In psychological research, the term variable usually refers to a feature upon which people can be assessed either in terms of some form of category (such as whether a person is married or single, or is employed or unemployed) or some form of value (e.g. that person's height, weight, exam results, or the time he or she takes to respond to a stimulus in a reaction time experiment).

As is the case with each of the above examples, all variables need to have more than one potential value in order for them to vary. Marital status, for example, needs to consist of the above two categories – or potentially even more, such as divorced or widowed – while a person's percentage score on an exam could take any one of a hundred different values. A characteristic or factor which does not have more than one possible value cannot really be treated as a variable and must be considered to be a constant.

Variables are generally classified in the following manner:

- *Independent*: The variable which is intentionally changed or manipulated by a researcher in order to determine the effects (if any) which this may have on the dependent variable.
- *Dependent*: The variable which is measured by a researcher, and which may (or may not) change as a result of the manipulation of the independent variable.
- *Control*: The variable which is held constant, so that the researcher can have a greater degree of certainty that changes in the dependent variable are indeed due to

changes brought about in the independent variable, rather than changes in any other factors which may influence the result.

* Confounding: Any variable which is not being manipulated or controlled, but which may have an impact on the measurement of the dependent variable. Such a variable is largely beyond the influence of the researcher.

For example, if we were to conduct a study investigating how exposure to aggressive images can influence young people's attitude toward the punishment of violent crime, we could construct scales to measure such attitudes and administer these to research participants before and after we had shown them a series of such aggressive images. We would then compare the before and after ratings to determine if there were any significant differences between the two.

Although very simple, this example is useful as an illustration of the aforementioned four types of variables. The dependent variable being measured here is the participant attitude toward punishment, as represented by the attitude scales being administered, while the independent variable being manipulated by the researcher takes the form of the actual exposure to the images. The main control variable being held constant in this scenario is that of age (as the study is concerned with the attitudes of young people), although in reality many other factors would be controlled for also. Finally, the confounding variables here could take many forms – just one example would be the uncontrolled exposure to aggressive images outside the study (e.g. the extent to which participants are exposed to such images on an everyday basis from sources such as newspapers and TV).

This classification of variables is essential for conducting research, as we need to have a clear understanding of just what it is that we are measuring, manipulating or holding constant – particularly with more complex research investigations. Further classification of how each of these variables can be measured, that is, their 'level' of measurement, is just as important for the purposes of effective data analysis. This will be outlined in the section below.

1.1 Variables and their measurement

1.1.1 Concepts

There are two ways in which variables are normally classified. The first refers to the level of measurement, which determines the degree of information available within the variable and the kinds of arithmetic operations that can be performed upon it. The level of measurement of variables in psychology is usually via the 'nominal', 'ordinal' and 'scale' categorization. The second approach to classifying variables refers to the relationship between different scores on that variable, that is, whether the variable is 'discrete' or 'continuous'.

Although these two aspects of variables are relatively straightforward, it is vitally important that they are fully understood from the outset as they form the basis of much of the rest of this book. In order to correctly interpret the results of any statistical test or procedure, such as those discussed in later chapters, we need to be sure that the correct test or procedure is used – the choice of this test being directly based on the nature of the variable being studied. Some procedures which are suited for use with continuous data need not be suitable for data defined as discrete. Similarly, some procedures used with data of a scale level of measurement should not be used with data which are classed as a nominal variable. To do so would simply result in the wrong results and with incorrect conclusions being drawn.

Nominal, ordinal and scale

There are generally considered to be three levels of measurement used in psychological research, known as 'nominal', 'ordinal' and

'scale'. With nominal measures, we are able to categorize participants according to their differences, but we cannot say to what
extent or to what degree they differ. Similarly, we cannot rank
them or place them in any form of order. The term *nominal* is
derived from the word 'name', and this is essentially all we can do
with this form of variable – that is, name the variable and then
count how often we can apply that 'name' to participants. *Ordinal*
measures provide additional information to that of nominal, as
they permit the *ordering* of individual scores. We are able to not
only differentiate cases from one another, but to also place these
in an increasing or decreasing order. *Scale* data adds to that of
ordinal data, as it incorporates additional information regarding
the degree of difference between individual items within a set or
group. In the case of scale data, we can place each score precisely
along a given scale, and determine exactly the size of the intervals between those scores. It is due to this equidistant nature of
the scale of measurement that we can also add, subtract, average
and generally manipulate the data in ways which are simply not
possible with the aforementioned nominal and ordinal levels of
measurement.

Discrete and continuous

In addition to the levels of measurement approach to categorization, variables can also be classified by referring to the relationship
between the data or scores which are collected. This relationship
takes one of two essential forms – that which is based on either a
'discrete' or 'continuous' scale. A *discrete* scale is one in which individual scores are independent of one another, and which involve
only 'whole' numbers. Scores on a *continuous* scale, however, can
be situated anywhere along a continuum, and can take the form
of not only whole numbers, but also of fractions.

The discrete and continuous aspects of variables and their measurement are usually considered alongside the aspects of nominal,
ordinal and scale rather than separately. By considering both of
these aspects together, we are better able to fully appreciate the
nature of the variable under investigation, and to then select the
most appropriate method by which it should be analysed. It may
be useful to consider the following rules of thumb concerning
the relationship between the two aspects – (1) nominal data will

always be discrete, (2) ordinal data will always be discrete, (3) scale data may be either discrete or continuous.

It may be worth adding here that measurements taken of a continuous variable are considered as approximations, at least in the way that they are reported – in other words they are 'rounded up' to the required number of decimal places. For example, a reaction time of 352.5505 ms may be rounded to 352.551, or 352.55, or 352.6, or 353, depending on the degree of accuracy required. A discrete variable, on the other hand, is more definite and does not normally require this rounding up procedure. For example, the recall of ten items in a memory test is just that – ten items – and needs no further approximation or adjustment.

1.1.2 Everyday examples

One of the most frequently used classifications in psychological research, and also a categorization of people that we tend to use on an everyday basis, is that of the sex of the participants in a given study. This is usually denoted as M or F for obvious reasons. This is the classic textbook example of a nominal level of measurement, along with other – often sociodemographic – factors such as married or single, and employed or unemployed. Such variables are considered to be nominal as they are mutually exclusive (one cannot be simultaneously married and also single), and as they offer no indication of order (one cannot say that married is 'higher' than single, or that indoors is 'lower' than outdoors).

One of the most important features to remember when dealing with nominal data is that it is just that – nominal (i.e. not numerical). This can sometimes be overlooked when numbers rather than letters are used to indicate categories. Although men and women are often classed or coded in research as 'Category M and Category F', this could just as easily be coded as 'Category 1 and Category 2'. In such cases, even though numerical codes are used, we are still restricted to simply counting the number of cases in Category 1 and Category 2. We cannot, for example, add one to the other and create Category 3! Similarly, it is still just as meaningless to regard one category as higher or lower than another. Taking a sporting example, we can see that the use of shirt numbers is used to distinguish the eleven members of a football team, but based on this alone it is meaningless to say that player number eight is higher or better than player number five.

Just as with the nominal data variable of 'sex', there are a number of classic textbook examples of the ordinal level of measurement. Perhaps the most frequent of these is the 'running in a race' analogy – or more precisely, the 'first past the post' analogy. If we were to stand near the finishing line of a race at its closing moments we may see the winner, the runner up, the runner in third place and so on, but the exact differences in finishing times between these three would be unknown without the use of a stopwatch. Indeed, whatever the time differences between the first, second and third position may be, they will still attain the status of first, second and third. Similarly with the results of a UK general election, we tend not to pay much attention to the number of votes cast, but we do know soon enough who forms the government, the opposition and who takes the third party position, regardless of the differences in the number of votes between them. The main point here is that, with ordinal data, there is no information of the distances between points on a scale – we simply know the order of those points, just as with the order of runners in a race or political parties in a general election – and furthermore that we cannot assume the distances between those points to be equal.

Ordinal measures may thus indicate the position of an individual in relation to others in that group, but because the data indicates order only and cannot assume equidistance, certain arithmetic decisions would be meaningless. For example, we cannot add first and second place to make third place! Furthermore, because we cannot know the size of the gaps between each person in the race, we can say nothing about how much faster one was than the others.

Ordinal data is most often found in psychological research in areas such as attitude measurement, where a participant indicates his or her position on an issue on a scale of, say, one to five (where one would indicate strongly disagree, five indicates strongly agree, and the numbers between indicating points between these two extremes). It may be tempting for researchers to manipulate these data (ones, twos, threes and so on) by adding, subtracting or averaging, but it should really be remembered that these are still numerical codes assigned to categories, rather than actual numbers, and therefore that such manipulation should be avoided.

In terms of scale data, a useful example can be found in psychological experiments on reaction time. As reaction time (and time in general) is measured on an equidistant scale, we can say that the interval between 310ms and 313ms is the same as that between 303ms and 306ms. This is due to the duration of the 3ms difference in each case always being the same. This is in contrast to ordinal data, where the length of the gap between the third and the sixth persons past the post may be very different from the gap between the tenth and thirteenth persons past the post (even though there is the same 'distance' of three persons in each case).

Reaction time experiments also offer us an example of a continuous level of measurement, as their results are recorded along a continuous scale. Similarly, measurements of height and weight are also recorded along a continuous scale of measurement. In practice this is clearly visible when there are numbers to the right of the decimal point, such as with a reaction time of 320.25 seconds, or a participant's weight being measured at 82.43 kilograms, or their height being recorded as 1.78 metres.

Discrete variables, on the other hand, will have no such fractional values or numbers to the right of the decimal point. Simple examples of discrete variables could include classification of family size according to the number of children in a family – this would be considered discrete since it is impossible to physically have one and a half or two and a quarter children. Similarly, data recorded on athletes' performance in the aforementioned race would also be discrete, as although there may be runners in first second and third position (i.e. positions 1, 2 and 3), there will be nobody recorded as being in position 1.5, 2.5 or 3.768.

One last point to make before we move on to consider actual research studies which illustrate the aforementioned aspects of variables concerns the relationship between the two aspects (i.e. discrete/continuous and nominal/ordinal/scale) of such variables. As mentioned toward the end of 1.1.1, we should remember that (1) nominal data will always be discrete, (2) ordinal data will always be discrete and (3) scale data may be either discrete or continuous.

Hopefully the reasons for this have now become a little clearer – we cannot measure either nominal or ordinal type variables on a continuous scale, simply because the resultant measures cannot be broken down into fractional units. We cannot, with ordinal data for example, record the position in a race as being between first and second – the athlete would be either in position 1 (first) or position 2 (second), and thus a fractional value (e.g. 1.5) could not apply. Similarly with nominal data, categorizing participants by sex would always result in either a value of 1 (e.g. Male) or 2 (e.g. Female), and again a fractional value (e.g. 1.5) could therefore not apply.

Data measured on a scale level of measurement, however, can exist as both discrete and continuous. Reaction time, weight and height are all examples of continuous scale data, with such possible measurements as 356.25 ms, 85.24 kg, or 1.76 m. The number of items recalled in a memory experiment or the number or errors recorded in a spelling test, however, would represent discrete scale data, as it would be not be possible to recall, say, three-and-a-half items from memory, or to make 6.23 errors on a test, even though the points on the scale of items recalled or errors made will always be equidistant.

1.1.3 From the literature

The concept of variables and level of measurement are firmly embedded not just within psychological research but within the history and development of the discipline itself. Let's consider firstly the level of measurement and the discrete/continuous categorization.

The nominal level

Perhaps the most frequent use of the nominal level of measurement in psychology is found in the categorization of participants into males and females, that is, classification via the variable of sex. However, the use of the nominal level of measurement is obviously not limited to the consideration of results just in terms of the male–female divide, but can include many other factors of a mutually exclusive nature, such as race, geographical location, nationality or personality type.

One such study incorporating the measurement of several nominal category variables was that conducted by Piliavin, Rodin and Piliavin (1969). In response to growing public concern at that time over the reluctance of members of the public to assist or to come to at the aid of others (i.e. to engage in pro-social behaviour), Piliavin et el. set up an investigation which was conducted within train carriages on the New York underground. The researchers aimed to determine the factors which might encourage or discourage members of the public from assisting strangers who appeared to be in obvious need of such assistance. With this aim they planted a team of four students on the carriage of the train, one of whom acted as 'the victim', by feigning illness and collapsing. He remained in this state until he was either helped by a passenger or if this wasn't the case, until the train pulled in at the next stop where he was helped to exit the train by one of the other students in the team (known as 'the model'). The remaining two students acted as observers, positioned as discretely as possible in the carriage and recording the actions of the members of the public.

Piliavin et al. investigated the factors which may encourage helping behaviour primarily by varying the appearance of the victim. Sometimes the victim was played by a black student, sometimes by a white student. Sometimes the victim appeared drunk, sometimes he appeared sober. This variation therefore took place at the nominal level (i.e. black/white, drunk/sober). Similarly, the data being recorded by the two observers was also largely nominal, that is, they simply counted the number of citizens coming to the aid of the victim, the number moving away from the victim, and also noted a number of nominal features of the 'good Samaritan' such as their location within the carriage, their sex and their race.

Several years prior to the above investigation into bystander behaviour, Schachter (1959) conducted a famous investigation into the conditions under which people tend to affiliate, that is, to spend time in the company of others, in what has sometimes become known as his 'misery loves company' study. The main emphasis of this study was to investigate people's reactions to feelings of increased anxiety, specifically investigating whether people who feel anxious prefer to be left alone or prefer to have other people around.

Schachter proposed that increases in anxiety would cause increases in the desire to be with others, in other words an increase in the need for affiliation, and sought to investigate this via a relatively simple design. He thus established an experimental condition whereby student participants were told that they would be partaking in a study on the physiological effects of electric shock, and that as part of the study they would receive a series of shocks while their blood pressure was being monitored. Half of the participants were told that the shocks would be very painful, while the other half were told that the shocks would be absolutely painless. Two groups of participants were therefore given very different information specifically referring to the degree of pain they would be experiencing in the experiment which was to take place.

In reality, none of the participants received any electric shocks at all – they simply received this information on potential pain in order to provoke different levels of anxiety. After they were given this information on the levels of pain that they would soon be experiencing, the participants were told that there would be a short delay while the experiment was being set up, and were asked if they would prefer to spend the time waiting for the experiment to begin either in the company of other participants, or in solitary rooms. This choice of where to wait was the information that the experimenters were actually seeking, and once the participants had made this choice the data collection for the experiment was complete – as the real aim was simply to see whether participants who had received the 'scary' briefing were more likely to spend their time in the company of others if given the choice. This was indeed the case, with a significantly greater number of participants in the fright condition than the non-fright condition choosing to affiliate with others.

In each of the above studies, the level of measurement of the data being collected can be considered to be nominal as in each case the data consisted of simple counts of the numbers of people in each category, whether this be the number of people choosing to spend time in the company of others as with the Schachter study, or the number of people coming to the assistance of the victim as measured in the study of Piliavin et al.

It is also worth noting that the data collected in each of the above studies should be considered as being discrete. This is because in each case the data refer to numbers of participants in a given category, and as such cannot be further subdivided. For example, there may be three people in a particular category, but there will never be three-and-a-half people. Nominal data, therefore, should always be considered as being discrete.

The ordinal level

One of the areas of psychology in which ordinal levels of measurement are most frequently found is that of attitude research. The pioneering work of Festinger and Carlsmith (1959) on cognitive dissonance was based on the measurement of attitudes. This classic study required that participants engage in extremely boring tasks and to then be offered either a small or large payment for telling the next participant (who was actually an accomplice) that the task was really very interesting. In other words, participants were being paid to engage in counter-attitudinal behaviour, that is, of expressing a public opinion that a task was interesting while their private view or attitude was that the task was extremely tedious. Following payment, the participants attitude toward the tasks were measured via a Likert scale; each participant was given a series of statements relating to the positive experience of undertaking the task, such as 'I found the task highly stimulating' and asked to rate such statements on a 5-point scale of (1) Strongly disagree, (2) Disagree, (3) Neither agree nor disagree, (4) Agree, (5) Strongly agree.

The results of the study demonstrated a tendency for the boring task to be rated as more enjoyable and interesting by those receiving the lower rather than the greater payment, the theory here being that the participants in the low payment condition felt less justified to be telling untruths about the task as they were receiving less payment, or external reward, for so doing. Those in the lower payment condition were thus experiencing a greater level of dissonance (i.e. the uncomfortable inconsistency between one's attitudes and one's related actions) and in an effort to reduce the discomfort of dissonance, were adjusting their attitudes to more closely fit with their actions – in other words, convincing themselves that they were telling the truth by expressing an attitude that the task was more interesting than it actually was.

More detailed accounts of the Festinger and Carlsmith study can be found in most introductory psychology texts, along with many everyday examples of dissonance – such as the experience of those paying over the odds for a touted concert ticket (those paying more tending to rate the band's performance higher than those paying the standard fee – in order to reduce any dissonance felt concerning the extra cash being paid). Similarly, studies on everyday activities such as smoking have also revealed the strategies employed to reduce dissonance between actions (smoking cigarettes) and attitudes (e.g. of personal health risk) (McMasters and Lee 1991).

In a much more recent study into attitudes, Aron et al. (2000) conducted an investigation into the relationship between the actual behaviour and activities of marital couples and their attitudes toward, or levels of satisfaction with, the marriage. The researchers were primarily interested in finding out the extent to which engaging in exciting activities with a marital partner would relate to measures of relationship satisfaction. They determined this by conducting a survey to capture data on both these variables, and then compared the two resultant sets of scores, that is, the scores on exciting activities and the scores on marital satisfaction. The surveys were comprised of a number of question sets which included items such as 'in general, how often do you think that things between you and your partner are going well?' answered on a 6-point scale ranging from 1 (all of the time) to 6 (never) and 'how bored are you with your current relationship?' answered on a 5-point scale ranging from 1 (not bored at all) to 5 (extremely bored). The results of the study indicated that shared participation in novel and arousing activities was consistently associated with higher levels of relationship quality. In other words, that as engagement in exciting activities increased, so too did the positive attitudes toward, and the feelings of satisfaction with, the relationship itself.

Methodologically, the important thing to note here is that the data in both these studies were being measured on an ordinal level as there could be no guarantee that the difference between points one and two on the scale (i.e. the distance between strongly disagree and disagree) would be the same as that between points four and five on the scale (i.e. the distance between agree and strongly agree).

In terms of the discrete/continuous classification, the above studies were essentially collecting discrete data. Just as was the case with the nominal studies outlined previously, it would not be possible to further subdivide the data collected at the ordinal level of measurement, for example, to rate an attitude on a Likert scale as 2.5 or 2.53. Just as with athletes finishing a race in positions 1, 2 or 3 (i.e. in first, second or third) but never in positions 1.5, 2.6 or 3.7, so too is it the case that the points on the attitude scale are whole numbers, discrete units which have no further subdivisions.

The scale level

A frequently used example of a scale level of measurement used in psychology is that of the passing of time, whether this be measured in hours, seconds or milliseconds. Psychological research which is focused on the measurement of time can be rather varied. It can range from the measurement of the period of time engaged in a specific activity or task, as is the case with observational studies on the behaviour of children; it can include the time taken for specific information memorized under specific conditions to be forgotten, as is the case with research on item trace decay of short-term memory; or it can be found in areas of psycho-physiological research as in classic experiments on reaction time, that is, the time which elapses between the presentation of a stimulus and the onset of a response to that stimulus.

The earliest experiments on reaction time are usually credited to Donders (see Donders 1868), a Dutch physiologist interested in measuring the amount of time taken to perform basic mental processes. His early experiments involved electric shocks being applied to the right and left feet of participants, who were then required to respond by pressing a telegraph key with the corresponding right or left hand. An early variation of the experiment saw Donders establishing two experimental conditions, one where the participant was warned in advance which foot was to receive the shock, and one where no advance notice was given. The results suggested that those in the 'advance notice' condition did in fact react more quickly, by around a fifteenth of a second. Such measurements have been refined in reaction time experiments over the years (Donders and his contemporaries used a nineteenth-century innovation known as the Hipp Chronoscope for the research studies) but the basic form of measurement of reaction time experiments remains the same – that of time itself – recorded via a scale (actually ratio) level of measurement.

A more recent study concerned with measurements of time, and one which takes place within the very different arena of animal or comparative psychology, considered the time which an individual spent engaged in specific activities as its main focus. Alexander and Hines (2002) investigated the factors which could account for observed sex differences in toy preference, that is, whether male infants tended to prefer to play with masculine toys, with females preferring to play with feminine toys. However, in order to determine the biological influence in such toy preference, the researchers chose not to select the more familiar participants usually found in such studies (i.e. boys and girls) but rather selected male and female members of a species of monkey as their participants.

The researchers in this study used six toys as stimuli – two defined as masculine, two as feminine and two as neutral. The participants were introduced to the toys, and their activities and interaction with them was videotaped. The resulting recordings were then observed, and the amount of time which each participant spent with each of the toys, either in terms of the time spent in direct interactive contact or the time spent in close proximity to the toy, was carefully recorded. Interestingly, the results indicated that sex differences in toy preference with these nonhuman participants was indeed observed. That is, that the female monkeys spent a greater proportion of their toy contact time with feminine toys than did the male monkeys, and that the male monkeys spent a greater percentage of their toy contact time with masculine toys than did their female counterparts. From the methodological perspective, the important thing to acknowledge here is the nature of the variable being measured in this experiment, that is, that the amount of time spent with each toy can be considered as being on a scale level of measurement.

The data collected in both the Donders and the Alexander and Hines studies differ from those mentioned earlier not only in that they represent a scale level of measurement, with equal distances between the points on the scale being used (in this case points in the measurement of time), but they also differ in that the data points can be further subdivided. A monkey may play with a toy for two minutes, two and a quarter minutes or even 2.2532 minutes. Similarly, a participant's reaction time may be measured as 375 ms, 375.2 ms or 375.23 ms. The degree of accuracy or extent of 'rounding up' is largely a result of the choice made by the researcher.

As well as the level of measurement, we can also consider the aforementioned studies in terms of the variables being manipulated, measured and controlled. A quick glance at the above studies should enable us to see the independent variables being manipulated by the researchers and also the dependent variables being measured.

Independent and dependent variables

The independent variable in the study by Piliavin et al. (1969) was simply the appearance of the victim. This was manipulated by the researchers to establish two conditions, that the victim should come across either as a disheveled person who appeared to have been drinking or as a more soberly dressed person walking with the aid of a cane. The effects of manipulating the independent variable of appearance were measured in terms of recording the number of onlookers who assisted the victims in either condition, this number therefore representing the study's dependent variable. The independent variable manipulated in the Schachter (1959) study took the form of the type of information given to participants, as well as the general situation in which they found themselves. This was classed as being either of a high-anxiety (with the emphasis on stress and pain) or low-anxiety condition. The effect which this had upon the dependent variable, that is, the participants' desire for affiliation, was then measured by noting the proportion of participants in each of the high- and low-anxiety conditions who chose to wait with fellow participants.

The Festinger and Carlsmith (1959) study used the amount of reward being offered to participants, set at either a dollar or twenty dollars, as the independent variable. The effects of the exposure to each of these two reward conditions was then measured via the participants' responses on the Likert-type attitude scale, these expressed attitudes to the boring task undertaken by the students thus representing the dependent variable. The second 'ordinal' study outlined earlier, that conducted by Aron et al. (2000) incorporated two dependent variables, that is, marital satisfaction and engagement with activities which were defined as exciting or arousing. This study, however, was not based upon the manipulation of an independent variable, but was based on an examination of two existing dependent variables. The reasons for this will become clear when we discuss studies based on correlation, in Chapter 4.

In the Donders (1868) reaction time experiment, the manipulation of the independent variable took the form of the advance warning (or lack of) given to the participant. The effects of this on the dependent variable of reaction time was then measured by recording the time taken for the participant to react to the electric shock in each of these warning/no warning conditions. In the case of the Alexander and Hines (2002) study, there were actually two independent variables – although only one of these was directly manipulated. The first was the nature or gender identification of the toy, categorized as masculine, feminine and neutral; the second was simply the sex of the participants that is, male and female monkeys. This second factor may be considered by many psychologists not to be an independent variable at all, as the sex of the participants cannot be directly manipulated by the researcher, and rather than it be classed as an independent variable it would be considered as a naturally occurring variable. The effects of this investigation were measured by recording the time spent with each toy, this scale level of measurement thus comprising the dependent variable.

The main emphasis of the studies outlined in the last few pages can be neatly summarized as in Table 1.1:

Table 1.1 Illustrative studies in terms of their main methodological features

Study	Independent variable	Dependent variable	Nominal, ordinal, scale?	Discrete or continuous?
Piliavin et al.	Appearance	Assistance	Nominal	Discrete
Schachter	Anxiety	Affiliation	Nominal	Discrete
Festinger and Carlsmith	Reward	Attitude	Ordinal	Discrete
Aron et al.	N/A	(1) Activity (2) Satisfaction	Ordinal	Discrete
Donders	Warning	Time (reaction)	Scale	Continuous
Alexander and Hines	(1) Toy type (2) Sex	Time (spent in play)	Scale	Continuous

Control and confounding variables

While the independent and dependent variables in any given study should be relatively easy to identify, we sometimes need to look a little closer for the control and erroneous variables. In the case of control variables, we need to examine the research design in order to identify the variables which need to be held constant and thus need to be controlled in order that they do not interact or influence the dependent variable – as the measurement of the dependent variable should reflect the manipulation of the independent variable only. In the above studies, the control variables could include elements such as the actual location within which the research takes place (such as the same room being used for both the high-anxiety and the low-anxiety conditions in the Schachter experiment), the time of day that the research takes place (which was a feature of the Piliavin et al. study), or any activities or tasks which are being conducted by the participants (e.g. the monotonous task which was set in the Festinger and Carlsmith experiment). If any of these factors had not been kept constant, then this may well have had an unintended effect upon the dependent variable.

In the case of the Piliavin et al. study for example, if the data collection had taken place at different times of the day, such as during peak and then off-peak travel, then there would have been different numbers of bystanders present which may have had obvious effects upon the numbers coming forward to give assistance – and thus an effect upon the results of the study. In this example, if the factor of time of the day had not been controlled for then it would have represented a confounding variable, that is, any variable not being manipulated or carefully controlled that could have an impact upon the dependent variable being measured. Reaction time experiments in particular are well known for their confounding variables, as there are so many possible factors which may impact upon the reaction time scores. These may include environmental factors (such as the amount of light, background sound, temperature), physiological factors (personal levels of fatigue or arousal, age, manual dexterity and general health) and personal factors (previous experience of the research, previous experience with the equipment or expectations of the study) as well as many others. Researchers will attempt to control for as many of these as they can, but it is not always possible to cover everything, thus sometimes leading to the presence of confounding variables – in such cases the researchers should make all possible attempts to ensure that they are at least aware of such confounding variables.

1.1.4 Narrative

Now that we have armed ourselves with some knowledge of the basics of psychological research – the words 'some' and 'basics' are being used here as there is still quite a bit to come, this still being the first chapter! – we should be able to consider a hypothetical research scenario and interpret it a little more in terms of its research and design aspects than we would have done before starting the book (hopefully!). We should at least be now able to interpret any given research setup in terms of the variables being manipulated (independent) and measured (dependent) as well as their actual nature (nominal/ordinal/scale and discrete/continuous). Let's try it with the scenario below...

In recent years, Thursday nights have seen something of a surge in popularity with many pubs and clubs offering reduced priced entry, promotional drinks and happy hours. Some have viewed this as evidence of a social change – of a bringing forward and thus expansion of the traditional weekend activities. Hence the phrase 'Thursdays are the new Fridays' (Hafner 2005). Unfortunately for most people, Friday mornings retain their status!

This is a development which may well pique the interest of social, cognitive or even educational psychologists, who may be intrigued as to how this change in Thursday night status could impact more widely – for example, of how it may impact upon Friday morning functioning. In other words how clubbing on a Thursday impacts on how well we perform at work or university the following morning. One way to investigate the possible effects of this on cognitive functioning would be to run reaction time experiments with a student sample on such a Friday morning. Let us imagine a psychologist conducting such an experiment each Friday over a three-week period...

Week 1 could see the researcher administering a computer-based reaction time experiment to two groups of students. The first group had been previously allocated into a 'Thursday clubbers' experimental group, while the second was comprised of those who had drawn the metaphorical short straw by being randomly allocated into a 'stay at home' condition. For each group a computer-based task is set and the computer program records the exact reaction time in milliseconds – as is usually the case in reaction time studies – which the participants take to successfully complete these tasks. The resulting data therefore represent a scale variable, as reaction time being measured in milliseconds clearly conforms to the equidistant data points requirement of the scale level of measurement. Furthermore, the data recorded here is of a continuous nature, with each recorded score being able to be broken down further, or indeed rounded up, in accordance with the required level of accuracy, for example, to two, three or even four decimal places if required. Thus, when the researcher later summarizes the recorded scores of the participants he will need to use measures suitable for scale level data (see Chapter 2). Similarly when the time comes to compare the recorded scores of the two groups to determine any significant differences between them, he will need to select a test which also corresponds to this level of measurement (such as those detailed in Chapter 4).

If we continue our visualization of this Thursday–Friday reaction time investigation a little further, we can perhaps consider a small but very important change to the above procedure taking place the following week. The second week of data collection sees the researcher administering the same experiment to the same two groups of individuals – and indeed at the same location, with the same equipment and at the same time of day – all of whom had once again been randomly allocated into the same 'night in' and 'night out' conditions . This time however, a fault in the reaction time program means that the accuracy of reaction times given in milliseconds cannot be assured, and so the researcher does not have access to the actual values in milliseconds as he had done previously. It is still, however, perfectly possible to note the order in which students completed the task – who came first, second, third etc. – and to thus rank the positions across the two groups. This resulting data set would then, therefore, no longer represent a scale level of measurement but would be considered as ordinal level data – due to there being no guarantee of the distances between positions being the same. The data would now also be considered as discrete rather than continuous, simply because there could be no fractional values to record, that is, the scores could represent positions of one and two, but never represent a position of one and a half. Again, the ordinal nature of the data would have implications for both descriptive and inferential statistics, as detailed in Chapters 2 and 4 respectively.

If we now turn our attention to the final phase of this three-week period, we could perhaps imagine one further twist taking place, with the third week seeing the researcher attempting to simplify or streamline the data collection process. This time, rather than to record exact reaction times, as in Week 1, or to make a note of participants' rank-order positions in the experiment, as in Week 2, he simply categorizes students' results in terms of whether or not they completed the task within the allotted time limit. In other words, he classed participants in terms of either 'completed' or 'non-completed' categories, representing these simply as 1 and 0. As was the case with the previous week's data, the resultant scores this time could be considered as being discrete (e.g. there would be no score of 0.5) but would this time be categorized as nominal in terms of their level of measurement. Scores would be either 0 or 1 – not so much a case of the 'first, second and third past the post' analogy of ordinal data, but more a case of a 'finished the race or didn't finish the race' analogy. As a result of the amendments then, the data produced in Week 3 of the study would require very different (and more rudimentary) measures for the subsequent descriptive and inferential analyses.

Whatever the outcome of the above experiments, they do offer an illustration of how what is essentially the same research question and activity (an experiment set up to determine if Friday morning reaction times differ between Thursday night clubbers and non-clubbers) can be analysed in different ways depending on the level of measurement. This can be summarized as in Table 1.2.

This simple scenario should help to illustrate why an awareness of the level of measurement of a given variable is essential

Table 1.2 Aspects of the reaction time study in terms of types of variables and levels of measurement

Week	Independent variable	Dependent variable	Level of measurement
1	Thursday night activities	Reaction time	Scale, continuous
2	Thursday night activities	Reaction time	Ordinal, discrete
3	Thursday night activities	Reaction time	Nominal, discrete

for choosing the statistical techniques which can be applied to the data collected. This is the case for both descriptive and inferential statistics. As will be pointed out in Chapter 2, descriptive statistics depend on the effective summarizing of data, and this requires the correct measure to be applied to the correct level of measurement – the mean (as described in Section 2.1) cannot be used to find the typical value of nominal or ordinal data, for example. Chapter 4 will demonstrate why this also applies to inferential statistics, which require that measures, or tests, be applied to the type of data for which they are most appropriate – for example, a t-test (Section 4.1) can be used with scale data but not with nominal data. Applying measures or tests to data that are not appropriate for such tests can lead to very unreliable (if not meaningless) results!

1.1.5 Further reading

Holt, N. and Walker, I. (2009). *Research with People: Theory, Plans and Practicals*. Palgrave Macmillan. chapter 3.

Howitt, D. and Cramer, D. (2008). *Introduction to Statistics in Psychology 4th Edition*. Pearson Prentice Hall. chapter 1.

Howitt, D. and Cramer, D. (2008). *Introduction to Research Methods in Psychology 2nd Edition*. Pearson Prentice Hall. chapter 3.

Miles, J. and Banyard, P. (2007). *Understanding and Using Statistics in Psychology*. London: Sage. chapter 2.

One more thing... a note on terminology: interval, ratio and scale

It may be worth noting that the latter level of 'scale' can be further subdivided into categories 'interval' and 'ratio'. Both of these feature equidistant measurements along a scale, but the ratio level of measurement has the added feature of an absolute zero. The differences between interval and ratio levels of measurement can be best explained by referring to two scales with which we are all very familiar: temperature as measured in centigrade, and time as measured in seconds. Both of these feature points on their scales which are equidistant. And therefore they represent an interval level, but time as measured in milliseconds features an absolute zero whereas temperature measured on the centigrade scale does not. In practical terms, this means that we cannot record an event which lasts less than zero seconds, but we can record a temperature of less than 0°C. To put it another way, it is possible for an interval level of measurement to include minus values whereas with a ratio scale it is not. While the presence of an absolute zero is a very important feature on any given scale of measurement, in psychological research we are rarely required to make this distinction and even the most sophisticated of the inferential tests that we use rarely require the data to be at a ratio level of measurement. It is therefore becoming more commonplace within psychology to collapse the two categories of interval and ratio into a single category of 'scale'. This has been the approach used by the most widely used statistical analysis package SPSS, and so will be the approach used throughout this book.

1.2 Research design

1.2.1 Concepts

There are many aspects of research design which need to be fully understood before embarking upon a research study, such as the importance of randomization, control, counterbalancing and so on. However, due to space limitations and also due to the general orientation of this book being toward data analysis rather than research methods, we will focus upon just three aspects of research design here – those which are considered as being the most crucial concepts to understand in order to perform analyses on quantitative data. In other words, this section will cover the aspects of research design that you will need to know before proceeding with the remainder of this book, that is, of being able to determine if research is *experimental* or *non-experimental*, and being able to see when a research design is of the *between* or the *within* variety.

In its simplest interpretation, an experimental research design is one that seeks to establish a cause-and-effect relationship, by manipulating an independent variable and measuring the effects which this may have on a dependent variable while striving to keep other factors constant. If all other factors are kept constant apart from the change being made in the independent variable, then any difference in the dependent variable can, theoretically, be attributed to this change in the independent variable. If we were to run an experiment to determine the preferred interface design of a social networking site, as may have been the case with the great Facebook revamp of 2008 (Shiels 2008), then we may set up a situation where a group of students performs a task on a PC with the first interface design, while another group performs the same task on a PC on which the second interface has been installed. The speed and accuracy of task completion on both systems could then be recorded. Assuming that we would be successfully controlling the experiment by keeping all other factors constant (e.g. environmental factors such as room heating and lighting, and participant factors such as age, manual dexterity and previous PC experience of the participants) then we would be investigating the effect which a single independent variable (interface design) has on two dependent variables (the speed and accuracy of task completion). In other words, we would be investigating a cause-and-effect scenario, of how changes in one, independent variable cause a change or an effect to take place in another, dependent variable.

A non-experimental research design, in contrast, does not seek to determine cause and effect in this way. Rather, it seeks to develop an understanding of the relationship between two or more variables without trying to establish any degree of causation. A non-experimental approach to the aforementioned investigation could be just as easily applied, but would not enable any cause-and-effect relationship to be established. For example, the researcher could adopt a survey approach to data collection, such as administering a questionnaire asking users to rate specific aspects of each interface design. Such a survey could elicit data on the ease with which users navigated the links of each version, or on how often they found themselves making mistakes or clicking the wrong links. Such an approach would represent a perfectly acceptable way of investigating this phenomenon – and may well show that, for example, those users of the second interface report a greater degree of user satisfaction than those navigating the first. However, it would not be able to uncover the cause-and-effect relationship between these variables as could the aforementioned experimental version.

For the purposes of understanding the similarities and differences between the various research designs, it may be simplest to consider the above in terms of the following three categories (which closely reflect the analysis procedures we will encounter in later chapters).

Experimental: Between: The between groups design – also known as between participants or between subjects design – refers mostly to experimental studies where the different conditions of the experiment are comprised of different participants. In other words, two or more different groups of people each undergo procedures or treatments which comprise different levels of the independent variable. This design is also referred to as an unrelated or an independent measures design. The two groups are usually formed by the use of a randomization procedure, that is, the participants from the whole sample are randomly assigned to either one group or the other, such that there is equal likelihood that a given participant will be allocated to one group as to the other. This is an important step in ensuring that the two groups are comparable at the onset of the experiment.

Experimental: Within: In contrast, the within groups design – or within participants, or within subjects design – usually refers to experimental studies where the same participants are to be found in the different conditions of the experiment. In other words, the same people undergo procedures or treatments which comprise the different levels of the independent variable. This design is also referred to as a paired, repeated measures, or related design. Randomization is also normally applied here, only this time not in terms of the allocation of the participants into one or other condition, but in terms of the order in which the treatments are applied.

Correlation: The correlation design is something of a departure from the above. This is, for the most part, considered as a within participants design where there is no controlled intervention. It therefore differs from the experimental designs in that there is no independent variable involved. Rather, individual participants are measured on two separate dependent variables, and the results of these measurements are examined to determine any significant similarity, or indeed significant *dis*similarity, between them.

1.2.2 Everyday examples

One area where 'between' research is frequently employed, and with which you may be familiar (although not as familiar as your lecturers) is the annual exercise conducted in universities of assessing the current year's exam performance in relation to that of the previous year. This can be undertaken for the purposes of quality control and to alert the department if there is any possibility that significant differences between annual cohorts might be due to unforeseen events. However, this procedure is also sometimes undertaken in a more controlled manner in order to determine the impact of an intentional intervention, such as the introduction of a new text or new assessment criteria. In such circumstances, the student performance figures of last year, such as the mean score and standard deviation, could be noted at the end of the academic year in July, the intervention (such as introducing a new essential text) could be made in October, and the effects of this – gauged by noting the end of year exam results and comparing these to those of the previous year – could be determined via the use of the appropriate statistical test (in this case probably via the independent t-test which will be covered in Chapter 4). Such an investigation would be considered as a between-participants design as the cohort of last year, apart from the odd 're-sitter', would be comprised of an entirely different set of people than the cohort of the present year. In other words, there would be different participants in each of the conditions.

The 'within' experimental design is perhaps most commonly found with 'before and after' scenarios. Indeed the words 'before' and 'after' are key words to look out for when reading and interpreting questions in statistics assignments. Examples within psychological research include studies which examine psychological changes that are brought on as a result of a physiological intervention – assessing the effects of a well-known recreational drug on short-term memory, for example. One potential approach here would be to ask participants to memorize a list of random numbers and to report these verbally and as accurately as is possible. The intervention would then take place (i.e. the substance would be administered), with the participants then being required to memorize and recall a list of comparable random numbers. As the numbers would be comparable and the participants the same in each condition (and all other relevant factors kept constant) we would attribute any change in the extent of recall as being due to the physiological intervention, that is, the introduction of the drug. To assess whether there was any change between the before and after condition, we would therefore use an appropriate within groups test.

Most of us probably have a fairly well-developed 'common-sense' understanding of correlation – essentially based on the notion that if some events take place then other events seem to take place too. If we consider the weather, for example, we may observe that people tend to wear sunglasses more in the summer than in the spring, and more in the spring than in the winter. As we know that the hours of sunlight increase from winter through spring to summer, we could see a positive correlation here, of increased sunglass usage taking place alongside increased hours of sunlight. Conversely, we might note that people, unsurprisingly, wear more clothes in the winter when the weather is cold than they do in the summer when the weather is hot. From this we could consider there to be a negative correlation – that as the temperature decreases, the amount of garments being worn increases.

A little closer to home, we may sometimes wonder why we have to attend so many lectures and read so many books on a given academic subject (such as statistics). Well, there are correlations involved here too, although this time of a positive nature – of the variables 'time spent in study' and 'marks attained in the final exam'. In other words, that as the time spent studying a given subject increases, the mark gained in an exam on that subject also increases – or at least we would hope so.

It may be worth noting here that positive correlation also occurs when values of variables decrease. In the above example, if we found that our exam results decreased following a semester where our hours of study also decreased, then this would still represent a positive correlation (even if the connotations of this appear quite negative). A negative correlation would take place if we found that our exams scores decreased after we had diligently been increasing our study inputs. Hopefully, such a scenario will never arise ...

1.2.3 From the literature

If we revisit the six studies outlined in Section 1.1.3, we should be able to identify the within-or-between nature of each by examining the structure of the variables and participants included in each group, or condition, of the independent variable.

In the study conducted by Schachter (1959), the independent variable was the level of anxiety, with two conditions being established, high and low. This therefore involved two separate groups of participants, those receiving the 'nice' and those receiving the 'nasty' treatment. As the participants were allocated to one group only – that is, either the high-anxiety group, or the low-anxiety group, then this study can be seen to be a between groups design. The Piliavin et al. (1969) study is also considered to be a between groups design. However, in the case of this particular study, we cannot be quite as certain of this, simply due to the nature and location of the data collection. As the research was undertaken in a natural setting, that is, the New York subway rather than in a lab, the researchers were able to exert a much lesser degree of control over the research environment. Although it was assumed that the bystanders in the subway during the exposure to the drunken victim condition were not the same individuals who would be exposed to the sober victim condition, this could not be taken as a certainty as the researchers had no control over those boarding or leaving the train. Admittedly, given the nature of the environment (the frequency of subway trains and the size of the population of New York), this would be seen as extremely unlikely. However, due to the lack of controlled lab conditions, the researchers could not have been completely one hundred per cent sure that the participants in the drunken condition were not also present in the sober condition.

The first study used as an example of the collection of discrete ordinal data (i.e. Festinger and Carlsmith 1959) also represents a between studies design as, just as with the examples above, the participants were allocated into mutually exclusive conditions. The conditions this time were based on the level of payment they received for describing the boring tasks as being interesting – either the dollar or the 20 dollars condition. Participants either received 20 dollars or received one dollar. As no participants were in receipt of both amounts this clearly identifies this as a between groups, or independent measures design. The second example involving ordinal data (Aron et al. 2000) is rather different. In this case, the researchers were not investigating differences between conditions or groups of people at all, rather they were examining the relationship between two separate variables in order to determine whether values on one variable could be seen to increase (or decrease) with values of another. Designs such as this are usually categorized as being related due to their very nature (see Coolican 2009 for a useful account of this).

The research designs of the two experiments discussed in the earlier section which were used to illustrate the scale level of measurement (with time as the dependent variable) were also quite different from one another. The Donders (1868) reaction time experiment can be considered as a related design as both treatments of the independent variable (i.e. the mild shock following the warning and mild shock following no such warning) were administered to the same participant. In other words, each participant was included in both conditions. The Alexander and Hines (2002) study, on the other hand, adopted a between groups design. The primate participants in the study were allocated into groups based on sex, and the time that each group (i.e. male and female monkeys) spent engaged with the various toys was recorded. These resulting times, or scores, could then be compared to determine if the time spent in play significantly differed between these two groups, and therefore whether there was actually a sex difference in toy preference among nonhuman participants.

The main emphasis of the last few pages can be neatly summarized as in Table 1.3:

Table 1.3 Illustrative studies in terms of their main methodological features

Study variable	Independent variable	Dependent variable	Level of measurement	Study type	Study design
Piliavin et al.	Appearance	Assistance	Nominal, discrete	Field	Between
Schachter	Anxiety	Affiliation	Nominal, discrete	Lab	Between
Festinger and Carlsmith	Reward	Attitude	Ordinal, discrete	Lab	Between
Aron et al.	N/A	(1) Activity (2) Attitude	Ordinal, discrete	Non-experiment	Within
Donders	Warning	Time (Reaction)	Scale, continuous	Lab	Within
Alexander and Hines	(1) Toy type (2) Sex	Time (spent in play)	Scale, continuous	Quasi	Between

1.2.4 Narrative

Earlier in this chapter we encountered the researcher interested in investigating the extent of 'that Friday morning feeling' (outlined in 1.1.4). If we return to this hypothetical scenario, we should now be able (with reference to the above sections if needed) to identify the fundamental nature of this research investigation and also its research design. In other words, we are now able to consider the research study not just in terms of variables and levels of measurement, but also in terms of its within-or-between nature, and of whether or not it could be considered to be an experiment.

Firstly, we can see that the research does conform to the requirements of an experiment. It incorporates an independent variable (Thursday night activity) with two levels, or conditions (either out painting the town red or staying at home). This independent variable was manipulated, via the researcher randomly allocating students into 'clubbing' or 'question time' groups prior to the Thursday night activities, in order to measure the effects of this manipulation on a dependent variable (the reaction times which were recorded on the Friday morning). Secondly in terms of the design, or the within-or-between distinction, we can see that participants were assigned to either a clubbing or a non-clubbing condition but not to both (i.e. different students were in different conditions). The design of the experiment should therefore be considered as being between – or which alternatively could be termed as an unrelated or independent measures design.

These aspects of the investigation could easily be modified if subsequent data collection sessions were held. For example, the design could relatively easily be adapted to the within variety (alternatively termed paired, related or repeated measures) as outlined in each of the three subsequent scenarios described below. Additionally, the form of the research study could also be changed from an experimental to a non-experimental investigation, as is the case with Week 6, below. Let's see how the researcher could modify the study in these ways by extending the research program to include an additional three Fridays worth of data collection...

Week 4 (as with Week 1 of the 1.1.4 scenario), could see the researcher administering the computer-based reaction time experiment to a group of students who had been partaking of the local nightlife the previous evening, that is, those same students who had been allocated to the clubbing condition of the independent variable just as before. As with the very first week of the study, the computer program records the exact reaction time of everyone in this group in milliseconds, and the researcher makes a note of this for the subsequent analysis.

Week 5 could then follow a similar pattern, with the very same group of students being invited along for the reaction time experiment. The same hardware and software would be used, the same instructions being given, and all taking place in the same location with the same environmental and controlled conditions. However, this time the data collection would take place during the morning after a relatively sedate night at home with only the panel of Question Time for stimulation. In other words, the participants of the 'night out' condition from Week 4 would also represent the 'night in' condition of Week 5. As before, the computer program records the exact reaction time of everyone in this group in milliseconds, and the researcher makes a note of this in preparation for the big day when the data analysis takes place.

When the analysis does take place, the researcher will be in the position of being able to compare the results of the Week 4 experiment with those of Week 5, and in doing so will be comparing a clubbing with a non-clubbing sample, aiming to determine if there are any significant differences in reaction time between them. The only difference between this scenario and that described in 1.1.4 is that this time the clubbing and non-clubbing samples are comprised of exactly the same individuals, whereas in scenario 1.1.4 these were two different groups of people. This is a very important distinction, not just in terms of practicality, logistics and cost of the research study, but also for the way in which the data is analysed (and the tests which are selected to enable this analysis to take place).

The changes to the original scenario could be extended even further, and could even move from an experimental to a non-experimental design. For example, Week 6 could see the researcher repeating the procedures of Week 4 – that is, when the participants attend the lab to undertake the reaction time program having spent the previous night out on the town. Thus, once again the same group attends on the Friday of Week 6, with the same computer program recording reaction times in milliseconds, and the researcher making a note of these as diligently as ever.

This time however, the researcher incorporates an additional element – he also asks the participants to indicate the actual length of time they were painting the town red the night before. He is thus employing a very different research design than he had been doing previously – instead of looking for significant differences between clubbing and non-clubbing conditions, he aims to examine exclusively the reaction times of the clubbing condition and to then determine if there is any relationship between these and the responses which the participants gave to the questionnaire. In other words, he is investigating the association between the time spent out on a Thursday night and the time 'spent' reacting to the stimuli of the experiment on the following morning. The aim this time, then, is to determine any significant similarity or correlation between these two sets of data – perhaps to see if increasing the number of hours spent clubbing on Thursday increases the length of time taken to respond in the reaction time experiment on a Friday (i.e. the longer the time spent clubbing the slower the participants will be). The researcher would thus test this hypothesis with a measure of correlation (in this case the Pearson Correlation Coefficient – see Section 4.1) rather than a test of difference as had been the case previously. It should be noted that Week 6 also differs in one other important aspect, in that this time there would be no independent variable, or at least not an independent variable which is manipulated in the same way as in the previous weeks. This is because the researcher is not allocating participants into either 'night in' or 'night out' conditions (all the participants on this occasion were spending the evening in town) nor is he allocating participants into survey or non-survey conditions (as all are completing the survey he has prepared).

Adding the Weeks 4, 5 and 6 of the study to our table first used in 1.1.4 (as in Table 1.4.) would therefore show how we can deconstruct an investigation or series of investigations in terms of their integral components – that is, of the design of the experiment (or non-experiment), the level of measurement of the dependent variable, and whether this be a discrete or continuous measure.

Table 1.4 Aspects of the reaction time study in terms of research design and levels of measurement

Week	Investigation	Design	Independent variable	Dependent variable	Level of measurement
1	Experiment	Between	Thursday activities	Reaction time	Scale, continuous
2	Experiment	Between	Thursday activities	Reaction time	Ordinal, discrete
3	Experiment	Between	Thursday activities	Reaction time	Nominal, discrete
4	Experiment	Within	Thursday activities	Reaction time	Scale, continuous
5	Experiment	Within	Thursday activities	Reaction time	Scale, continuous
6	Non-experiment	Within	Thursday activities	Reaction time	Scale, continuous

Awareness of all these elements is useful for understanding the nature of the research, but they are also essential for choosing the most appropriate statistical techniques to analyse the collected data, both in terms of descriptive and inferential approaches, as we shall see in the subsequent sections.

As mentioned at the start of this section, this brief account of research design is by no means comprehensive, and you are encouraged to read further on this topic, to include aspects such as randomization, counterbalancing, and the pros and cons of each of the above designs as well more complex 'mixed' and 'matched-pairs' designs (a design which may be considered either within-OR-between depending on the source you are reading). A more thorough coverage of these issues can be found in many good research methods texts. However, as these are relatively more complex issues – and as the fundamental aim of this first chapter is to prepare for the remainder of this guide – then we aren't going to go there! Hopefully, the above scenario and this chapter as a whole will have been reasonably intelligible, and if so should be sufficient to enable you to follow the two main chapters of this book, on descriptive and inferential statistics.

1.2.5 Further reading

Holt, N. and Walker, I. (2009). *Research with People: Theory, Plans and Practicals*. Palgrave Macmillan. chapter 3.

Howitt, D. and Cramer, D. (2008). *Introduction to Research Methods in Psychology 2nd Edition*. Pearson. chapter 9.

One more thing... a note on terminology: participants and subjects

There have already been several occasions throughout this first chapter where we have encountered a number of alternate expressions for the same concept. These include several terms which are entirely interchangeable, such as 'repeated measures', 'paired' and 'related' all applying to the within groups category, and similarly terms such as 'unrelated', or 'independent measures' for the between groups category. There are several other areas where alternate terms are used but not quite so frequently, such as in the case of nominal and scale variables being described as 'categorical' and 'cardinal', and the dependent variable being known as the 'response' variable. However, one term which is generally frowned upon these days is that of 'subject'. You may still find this in some of the older textbooks on research methods, but it has now generally been replaced by the term participant, largely due to the rather negative connotations which the word 'subject' can imply. Following concerns that such a term evoked images of the subject being a completely passive element in the research process, or even of implying a heavily unbalanced relationship between the subject and researcher (e.g. the oppressed subject being, well... 'subjected' to the will of the powerful ruler) the use of the term has steadily declined since the 1990s and has now virtually disappeared.

1.3 Summary

This first chapter has introduced us to the basic concepts which are essential for any research activity, that is, variables, participants and the notion of research design. Variables are the factors which we either manipulate or measure, or alternatively which we hold constant or at least try to acknowledge. We manipulate *independent* variables in order to measure the effect of such manipulation on the *dependent* variable of interest. In doing so, we try to ensure such measurements are indeed the result of our manipulation by holding *control* variables steady, or by recognizing and acknowledging the impact of the *confounding* variables which may have a detrimental effect on the above.

Each of the above variables, particularly the dependent variables being measured, are usually classified according to whether they exist only as whole numbers (discrete) or can be broken down further (continuous). Additionally, and crucially for the purposes of subsequent tests, variables are also classed as nominal, ordinal and scale – respectively based on their characteristics of mutually exclusive frequencies, order of magnitude and equidistant points on a scale.

The chapter has also outlined the basics of research design, a term which refers to the process by which the participants in any given investigation are measured in terms of the above types and levels of measurement, and a term which also refers to the orientation or arrangement of participants – usually in the form of either a between or a within groups design – in other words, of whether participants are randomly allocated between different groups each receiving a different treatment or level of an independent variable, or of whether participants are considered as a single group, with any measured differences (presumed to be due to the administered treatment) taking place within this single group.

Much more could probably be said about research design – taking in case studies and matched pairs scenarios, for example – as well as further and finer details being given on the characteristics of research samples and of the nature of measurement itself, as it is conceptually certainly not limited to the levels outlined above. However, for the purposes of this book, the initial chapter should hopefully have done its job – equipping us with the basic knowledge and understanding needed to progress to the next chapter, and to some actual data analysis.

1. Ordinal level data are characterized by:

   a. Data that can be meaningfully arranged by order of magnitude.
   b. Equal intervals between each adjacent score.
   c. A fixed zero.
   d. None of the above.

2. A Repeated Measures design would be appropriate for which of the following situations:

   a. A researcher would like to study the effect of alcohol on reaction time.
   b. A researcher would like to compare individuals from at least two populations.
   c. The effect of two new treatments, administered simultaneously on individuals with a rare condition.
   d. Both a and b.

3. Which of the following is a between groups design?

   a. All participants perform in all conditions.
   b. Each participant is tested twice, once in each condition.
   c. Different participants perform in each condition.
   d. None of the above.

4. What is the dependent variable in experimental research?

   a. A variable which nobody controls or changes.
   b. The variable which is manipulated in an experiment.
   c. The variable which is measured, to see results of an experiment.
   d. A variable which is held steady.

5. Temperature measured along the Fahrenheit scale can be considered as:

   a. Nominal data.
   b. Ordinal data.
   c. Scale data.

6. Participants take a simulated driving test twice, in one condition they have no alcohol, in the other they have enough alcohol to take them over the legal limit. Is this design:

   a. Repeated measures?
   b. Unrelated measures?
   c. Between subjects?
   d. Independent measures?

7. An experimental design in which all participants participate in all experimental conditions is known as:

   a. An Independent groups design.
   b. A Repeated measures design.
   c. A Matched groups design.
   d. An Unrelated design.

8. If a researcher wanted to investigate the effect of cigarette smoking by mothers on birth defects in children she would most likely conduct:

   a. An experimental study.
   b. An observational study.
   c. Correlational study.
   d. A case study.

9. A researcher investigates the effect of caffeine on sleeping behaviour by allocating participants into two groups, group 1 (drinking normal coffee) and group 2 (drinking decaffeinated coffee) before recording how long it takes participants to fall asleep. In this scenario:

   a. Time taken to sleep is the dependent variable and caffeine is the independent variable.
   b. Time taken to sleep is the independent variable and caffeine is the dependent variable.
   c. They are both independent variables.
   d. They are both dependent variables

2 **Descriptive statistics**

Where as the previous chapter was primarily concerned with establishing the *characteristics* of the data which are collected as part of the research process in psychology, this chapter (and for that matter the remainder of this book) will be aimed at shedding some light on what to actually *do* with that data. In other words, how we summarize, categorize, present, interpret and analyse that data. You should hopefully soon be able to see that without a knowledge of the former (i.e. the level of measurement, classification of variables, types of research design and so on) the latter (i.e. the actual analysis of the data) would not really be possible, or at least would not make a whole lot of sense.

Analysis of such data is normally undertaken via a two-stage process – essentially of firstly producing descriptive statistics and then following on from this with the production of inferential statistics – although it must be said that sometimes the calculation of descriptive statistics can indeed be an end in itself. These terms refer to the approach we take when analysing the data; whether we are simply summarizing the data in order to more clearly describe their characteristics (as is the case with descriptive statistics) or we are looking more closely at the data, in order to determine – or infer – any relationships which may exist (as is the case with inferential statistics). For example, calculating last year's average exam score on your research methods module, and the actual range of those exam scores from the highest to the lowest, would be considered as being part of a *descriptive* analysis. Comparing those results from last year's exam to those of the exam results from research modules of psychology degrees all across the UK, and then noting any significant differences between them, would be considered to be an *inferential* analysis. It should be noted, though, that just as with the quantitative–qualitative distinction, there is often some overlap to be found with descriptive and inferential statistics (Witte and Witte 2004: 5).

With an emphasis on how descriptive statistics are meant to summarize data, that is, convert a large dataset into something more meaningful and readily understandable, this chapter introduces the concepts of mode, median and mean (measures of central tendency) and also the concepts of range, IQR, variance and standard deviation (measures of dispersion). Any summary description of data should include *both* a central tendency and a dispersion measure to be meaningful. For example, knowing that the average score on the aforementioned first year statistics exam is 55% is all well and good, but it becomes much more meaningful if we are also aware of the range – or preferably the standard deviation – of scores. Knowing that this mean of 55% was calculated from scores which were mostly spread from 50% to 60%, say, creates a very different overall picture than that of a dispersion of scores ranging from 10% to 90%.

Following this consideration of the methods of central tendency and dispersion, the chapter then goes on to conclude with the various ways in which scores may be standardized, that is, via percentiles and Z-scores, and discusses the benefits which the use of standard scores can bring to gaining an enhanced understanding of a dataset prior to conducting any inferential analysis.

Summarizing findings via measures of central tendency

2.1.1 Concepts

The measure of central tendency within a dataset is quite simply its most 'typical' value. However there are a number of different forms of typical value used, depending mostly on the level of measurement of the dependent variable. These typical values are known as the mode, median and mean.

Mode

The simplest of the three measures of central tendency is the mode. The mode refers to the most frequent score of a given dataset, this frequency being the very reason why it is considered to be the most typical score (i.e. simply because it is the score that occurs most often). It is generally mostly associated with the nominal level of measurement – this being due to it representing the *only* measure of central tendency suitable to be used to summarize nominal data. However, the mode *can* also be used with ordinal or scale level data if so desired. One other point to note concerning the mode is that there need not always be a single mode within any given dataset. There might be two modes, known as a bimodal distribution, or several modes, known as a multimodal distribution – thus considerably limiting its use as a measure of central tendency in such cases.

Median

The median is typically used with ordinal data (although it is also frequently reported alongside the mean when summarizing data of a scale level of measurement) and refers to the score which is in the central position of any given dataset. Once all scores in a dataset are ordered in terms of their size or magnitude, the score in the centre – with equal numbers of scores on either side – is the median. It is therefore considered to be the typical value as it holds the very central position of a dataset. One point of note concerning the median is that, because it always effectively splits an ordered dataset into two halves, it is the value with a percentile rank of fifty. This may be useful to note when we encounter standard scores in Section 2.3. One final issue relating to the use of the median concerns the number of scores in a dataset – that we may need to exercise caution interpreting the median where there are relatively few scores. For example, in a set of five scores such as [1,1,2,78,89], we would have a median score of just two, and as almost half the scores are *way* more than this, it may be debatable just how typical this median value would be of the dataset as a whole.

Mean

The mode and median are obviously very straightforward concepts to grasp. The mean is also relatively straightforward, largely due to its widespread use, but on the other hand it is somewhat more sophisticated and its calculation requires a little arithmetic – although not too much! To determine the mean we simply add all the scores in a dataset and then divide that sum by the number of scores, for example, if we have half a dozen scores in out dataset then we add them all up and divide by six. As the mean is perhaps the most commonly understood measure of central tendency, it is the measure most frequently referred to as 'the average', or sometimes 'the arithmetic average'. For our purposes, we should note that it can only be used with data conforming to a scale level of measurement, and also that it forms the basis of many of the more sophisticated statistical procedures which we will encounter later in the book.

You may also note from various research methods texts that there are a number of different interpretations of the mean, for example, the references made to 'sample' and 'population' mean, as described more fully in Section 3.1. In order to differentiate these, it may be useful to know how these 'sample' and 'population' means are denoted in the literature: the sample mean takes the form of $\bar{X}$ (known as ex-bar), while the population mean is represented by the Greek character μ (known as mu).

One final point regarding the mean concerns its potential to mislead. It should be noted that, of the three measures of central tendency used in psychological research, the mean is the measure which is the most susceptible to extreme scores and thus most likely to give a misleading or distorted picture – and this does sometimes occur in the psychological literature (see the case of Buss and Schmitt 1993, below, for an example of this). However, as stated above, the mean is usually the most preferred measure of central tendency in psychology, and forms much of the basis of the whole area of parametric statistics.

2.1.2 Everyday examples

One of the traditional examples for illustrating the importance of the mode – and which was at one time popular as a GCSE question – relates to shoe size. This is based on the scenario of the owner of a shoe shop deciding to take a 'scientific' approach to replenishing the stock. Over a period of time, he makes a note of the shoe sizes of every customer who comes along to try on a pair. He then calculates the average (mean) shoe size and buys a truckload of shoes of this size thinking that he is more likely to sell pairs of this most typical size than any other. The obvious flaw in this strategy is that he should have used the mode, as this was a more realistic reflection of true customer requirements. Take for example, a sample of ten shoppers, half of whom were size four, two of whom were size six, and the remaining three were size seven (i.e. 4,4,4,4,4,6,6,7,7,7). Using the mean as the typical value of the sizes would have led to an average size of five – a shoe size which would not, of course, have suited a single shopper or led to a single sale. This legendary illustration of the mode still finds its way into a number of current texts, and can even be found in areas such as economics and sales forecasting (Lee, Lee and Lee 2000). Examples of the mode can often be found in the popular press, within articles discussing the number of people represented in mutually exclusive categories such as nationality or age group – such as the most frequent users of mobile internet devices being in the 16–24 age category, for example (Pollard 2007).

The median is frequently found in the social sciences when measuring quantities of an ordinal nature, such as assessing our opinions or attitudes toward a wide variety of issues, which could include government spending policy, levels of confidence in the banking system or perceived likelihood of health benefits resulting from the introduction of the law banning smoking in pubs. Such measurements are often incorporated within opinion polls with, for example, participants being asked to respond on a 5-point rating such as 'strongly agree to strongly disagree' to statements of the form 'I think the government is doing a good job' or 'I still think Big Brother is entertaining'. The results of such studies along with the associated median responses to such statements can often be found in the media, on areas such as racial prejudice (McVeigh 2001) and students' opinions of their university – elicited via the now legendary NSS national student satisfaction survey (Smithers 2005).

The main point to remember here is that although some of the areas of interest to surveys concern concepts associated with a *scale* level of measurement, the opinions or attitudes held by respondents toward these issues are *ordinal*, and thus the most effective form of a typical value here is the median. For example, a survey may ask questions to elicit participants' attitudes toward hospital waiting times or increased taxation or reduced financial support toward university fees. Each of these issues concern scale level variables (i.e. money and time) but participants' attitude toward them should be considered as ordinal. We also need to acknowledge, however, that the median may *also* be used alongside the mean when summarizing scale variables (such as the aforementioned taxes and waiting times), since scale level data can make use of all three measures of central tendency, and supplying more than one measure of central tendency can help to give a clearer overall picture.

The mean is a much more familiar concept to most of us than is the median or mode. Examples of the mean are to be found almost everywhere, as it is the most popular form of 'typical' value in general usage. Economists may regularly use the mean to report average earnings, health officials may use this as a measure of average hospital waiting times, and educationalists may apply it to the average number of GCSE passes of school leavers and so on. There is no denying its widespread use, but in using the mean, one should be aware of its drawbacks, such as the distorting effects it can have when there are just one or two extreme values included within the dataset. This is illustrated via the 'doubling the average income' example included toward the end of Section 2.1.2.

We can consider each of the three measures of central tendency further, particularly as regards the way in which each can be used, by considering the following everyday scenarios (well, perhaps not exactly everyday scenarios, but certainly those which should be somewhat familiar ...).

Firstly let's consider the changes which have taken place over the last few years within the world of music. Recent developments in this arena – such as the growth of internet-based file sharing, the emergence of Spotify-like media streaming (Topping 2009) and the apparent decline of the popularity of the CD as the media of choice – have led to some bands dabbling with innovative ways of spreading their message. This has included not just legal per-track downloads and cutting out the middleman (i.e. selling direct to consumers without a record company) but also even to letting the customer decide how much to pay. This was perhaps most prominent with the 2007 Radiohead release of *In Rainbows* (Pryor 2007).

Unsurprisingly, when this idea was first floated there was considerable interest in how much cash people are indeed willing to pay for an album in this way, but many of the media reports have been rather ambiguous, with a typical payment of £4.00 being quoted (Sherwin 2007) – but to what form of typical payment does that refer? Could it be the mode, median or mean? In other words, does it imply that the most frequent sum of all the various amounts paid was £4.00 (the mode), or that when all payments for the download were placed in sequential order from lowest to highest, the mid point was found to be £4.00 (the median), or that when all the money paid was taken into account and divided by the number who actually bought the album, the final figure was £4.00 (i.e. the average). Whether this figure was the mode, median or mean could have quite different implications for estimating the success of the 'pay whatever you like' strategy.

We could also consider the measures of central tendency by reflecting on the types of political or financial news stories we hear about everyday. Public opinion of MPs, for example, appeared to hit an all-time low during the expenses scandal which covered the front pages of many newspapers during the spring of 2009 (see PoliticsHome 2009). However, perhaps one could cynically say that confidence in this area has never been especially high, and that Governments may indeed be sometimes accused of 'fiddling the figures' to make themselves look more effective and efficient, or to make the economy look more healthy than it actually is. While we are all sure that no MP would never ever even dream of doing such a thing (!), we can, as data analysts, look at things critically to enable us to see the bigger picture. An example of this can be found in the case of average earnings...

Within our society, and most others for that matter, annual income is not normally distributed (see Section 3.3 for an explanation of this concept of normality). Rather, it is positively skewed, meaning that its income is clustered mostly toward the *lower* end of the pay scale. In simple terms, we can consider that this skewed distribution means (1) that most people earn low to moderate levels of income, (2) that a few people earn quite a lot, and (3) that a very small number of very lucky individuals earn huge wads of cash! The uneven distributions of salaries means that the average wage earned can fluctuate markedly simply by adjusting the amount of money that just a few people earn. Perhaps the following example, adapted from Miles (2001) can illustrate this.

Let's consider the average incomes of a sample of one hundred people. If ninety-nine of these earn ten grand per year, and one person earns a cool million per year, the mean amount of money earned is just under twenty thousand per annum (i.e. £19, 900 – or 1.99 million divided by a hundred). If the pay of the person earning that cool million is doubled, then the mean pay becomes just under thirty thousand (i.e. £29, 900 – or 2.99 million divided by a hundred). The powers that be could then say that, based on this sample, the average person has had a pay rise of around 50% percent (from just under twenty to just under thirty grand per year) even though 99% of them have had no extra cash whatsoever and remain firmly on the ten thousand figure. In other words, thanks to a millionaire becoming a multimillionaire, we can all rest assured that our average wages are on the increase – even though we're not actually seeing any of it!

This simple illustration shows how the use of the mean can have a distorting influence, and how using the median or mode as a measure of central tendency in some circumstances may allow us to see things from a quite different (and perhaps more realistic?) perspective. Interestingly, although the government tends to quote the mean when talking of wage increases such as that above, they often prefer to use the median when discussing issues such as child poverty or the minimum wage (Miles and Banyard 2007: 34).

2.1.3 From the literature

Many studies in psychology have made use of the mode as a measure of central tendency, although the actual reporting of the mode in the publications of the findings often tends to be overshadowed by that of the results of the inferential analyses. Nevertheless, the mode is very often the starting point of the data analysis for many studies, particularly those studies oriented toward a nominal level of measurement. A brief outline of two such studies is included below: the first, a classic lab experiment investigating the bystander effect (Darley and Latane 1969); the second, a field experiment considering factors in crowd conformity (Milgram and Toch 1969).

The Darley and Latane study was one of many conducted in the late 60s with the aim of exploring the nature of altruism or helping behaviour. The researchers designed the experiment such that participants would be housed in individual cubicles which were connected by an intercom. These participants were then required to engage in a discussion via this intercom system with groups of various sizes. Early in the discussion, a participant who was actually an experimental accomplice mentioned that he was prone to seizures. Later in the discussion, the same accomplice feigned a severe seizure and cried out for help. The researchers found that the tendency to help the apparent seizure victim declined as the size of the discussion group increased. The researchers constructed the experiment such that the number of people, or 'bystanders' present (i.e. the size of the discussion group itself) represented the independent variable, with this being composed of several levels, that is, one bystander present, two bystanders present, four bystanders present and so on. The dependent variable then, was the frequency of response to the cry for help. The level of the independent variable which produced the most frequent offer of help was found to be that of the single bystander. In other words, the greatest likelihood of the person in need of help actually receiving that help was found to occur when there was just one other person present. This 'single bystander' category thus represented the mode, or modal value of this study.

A study of the same period which investigated similar phenomena of the actions of individuals in relation to varying group sizes, although one which was conducted as a field rather than as a lab experiment, was that of Milgram and Toch (1969). This experiment examined the impact of 'precipitating' groups (named as such due to their function of precipitating a reaction from those around them) of varying sizes on the action of crowd formation. Groups made up of various numbers of accomplices were, in random sequence, positioned on a busy street in New York City with the members of the group performing the clearly observable action of looking up at the window of a building for a set period of time. The researchers recorded the scene in order to later take note of the number of bystanders who imitated the action, that is, the number of passers-by who also paused to look up at the window. Similarly to the Darley and Latane study, the independent variable being manipulated (and thus representing its levels or conditions) was the size of the group, with the dependent variable being the number of bystanders who 'joined in'. The researchers found that when group sizes ranged from one to five, the most frequent responses or reactions of the passers-by to the group activity occurred when the group was at its largest. In other words, the 'five member' category therefore represented the mode.

If we move on from the mode to the median, we could consider a couple of studies from the 1990s which provide an interesting interpretation on the use of the median versus the use of the mean. Both studies were concerned with the extent to which men and women differ in terms of their mating habits, or at least in terms of their *intended* mating habits, each study drawing on earlier research (such as Trivers 1972) which found that males generally invest more time and effort toward mating (and less time and effort at parenting) than do females.

The first study, by Buss and Schmitt (1993) found that men reported preferring more sexual partners than did women over various intervals ranging from six months to life that is, there was a notable sex difference between the stated preferred numbers of sexual partners. They reported this as being consistent with the evolutionary and biological view of the most effective strategy for genetic propagation – of women focusing on child rearing and of men seeking many partners due to their being able to produce a greater number of offspring than women for a much longer period of time.

The second study (Miller and Fishkin 1997) was undertaken in an attempt to further examine these findings, and indeed found similar results in terms of the mean numbers of preferred partners. However, when the median was employed as a measure of central tendency rather than the mean the results looked quite different. They found the average (mean) number of future partners desired by women over a proposed thirty-year period to be 2.8, while the corresponding figure for men was found to be a whopping 64.3. Such a difference would certainly seem to support the evolutionary/biological line outlined above. However, when the medians were calculated, they resulted in much more comparable (and perhaps much more realistic?) results, that is, of a median value of just two partners for both men and women.

Miller and Fishkin proposed that the findings in the previous study, that is, of the significant mean-level sex differences in the desire for a large number of partners, were misleading due to the presence of male outliers. In other words, due to just one or two males stating their somewhat enthusiastic desires for large numbers of future sexual partners (in excess of a thousand!), the mean for the male participants had been raised by a considerable degree. By focusing on the median values rather than the means, Miller and Fishkin removed the impact of these outliers and concluded that most men and women were actually fundamentally alike in their mating desires, with both wanting comparable numbers of partners over the course of a lifetime. Similar results were obtained by Pedersen et al. (2002), who also employed the median as the measure of central tendency.

2.1.4 Narrative

Let's return now to our previous scenario (as discussed in Sections 1.1.4 and 1.2.4), of our enthusiastic researcher determined to establish the after effects of Thursday evening happy hours on the student population. We are already aware of the different approaches he has used over the weeks, including both within and between research designs, collecting data of nominal, ordinal, and scale varieties, and with both an experimental and a non-experimental approach. Having now been introduced to the concept of central tendency, we should be in a position to establish what the initial forms of analysis of the data should be – that is, of which descriptive statistics the analysis should produce. If we revisit the previous summary table (Table 1.4) as a reminder, we should be able to quickly identify which forms of 'average' will be calculated for the data collected each week.

For the first and also final three weeks of the data collection, the level of measurement each time was scale, and so the most appropriate measure of central tendency to be used to summarize these data would most likely be the mean. For Weeks 2 and 3 however, we would most probably employ the median and mode respectively, as the former was based on the collection of ordinal data (as in recording the participants who were positioned as first, second and third to finish the task) while the latter reduced the complexity even further by collecting data of the nominal variety (i.e. the number of participants falling into two mutually exclusive categories). Our week by week summary could therefore be expanded to include a further column, as illustrated toward the end of Section 2.2 in Table 2.2 (although note the omission of the independent and dependent variable columns, removed to avoid repetition, as these remain the same over the entire six-week period). It should be acknowledged though that the data collected in Week 2 could also be analysed in order to produce a mode as well as a median, and that the data from Weeks 1, 4, 5 and 6 could also be summarized via mode and median as well as mean. Such are the extended possibilities when collecting data along a scale level of measurement.

Section 2.1. will hopefully have given a useful overview of what is usually the first port of call when performing analyses of any given dataset, that is, of establishing its most representative or typical value. However, as previously mentioned, any descriptive statistics requires not just a measure of central tendency but also a measure of dispersion – these will be addressed in the following section.

2.1.5 Further reading

Field, A. P. (2005). *Discovering statistics Using SPSS (and Sex, Drugs and Rock 'n' Roll) 2nd Edition*. London: Sage. sections 1.3, 1.4.

Holt, N. and Walker, I. (2009). *Research with People: Theory, Plans and Practicals*. Palgrave Macmillan. chapter 3.

Howitt, D. and Cramer, D. (2008). *Introduction to Statistics in Psychology 4th Edition*. Pearson Prentice Hall. chapter 3.

Miles, J. and Banyard, P. (2007). *Understanding and Using Statistics in Psychology*. London: Sage. chapter 2.

2.2 Summarizing findings via measures of dispersion

2.2.1 Concepts

An awareness of the typical value of a set of scores is undoubtedly very useful, but in order to obtain a true picture of the data that have been collected we also need to know something about the *distribution* or *spread* of the scores. The measure of the distribution of scores within a dataset establishes its pattern, and the extent to which individual scores can be considered as being low, high, central and so on in relation to all the others.

Range and interquartile range

The simplest (and least used) measure of dispersion is that of the range, which refers to the span between the minimum and the maximum of a given set of scores. It is thus simply the difference between the lowest and the highest values in a dataset. The problem with the range is that in telling us the minimum and maximum of a set of scores, it tells us nothing of how the scores are arranged between these two extremes, of whether most scores are for example to be found near the minimum, the maximum, or whether they are more evenly distributed. The interquartile range (or IQR) is generally preferred to the range as a measure of dispersion, as it concentrates on the central 50% of scores. It eliminates the lowest 25% and highest 25% of scores from the descriptive analysis, thus leaving just the central two quarters (or 50%) to be taken into account. It is thus considered to give a greater focus on the dispersion of 'typical' scores. The value of the interquartile range is thus much less distorted by extremely low or high scores than is the range. However this is still not the dispersion measure of choice, as it still does not take all the scores in a dataset into account.

Variance

Although its calculation is more complex than that of the range or IQR, the variance is just another way of looking at the distribution of scores, but with a focus on the mean – it simply measures how widely spread the values are in relation to the mean. If most scores in a given dataset are similar to the mean score, then the variance is said to be small. If many scores are distant from the mean score, then the variance is said to be large – and if all scores are exactly the same as the mean, then the variance is zero! To calculate the variance, we work out how far each score is from the mean (i.e. the *distance* between each score and the mean score), and then add all these distances together. Sounds simple enough so far! We do, however, require one extra step, due to the way that scores are found both above and below the mean. Since scores below the mean are given minus values, and those above the mean are given positive values, if we simply added all the distances together then those values below the mean would cancel out those above. The extra step required is therefore to *square* the distances before adding them all together. This removes the negating effect of any minus values (since multiplying a minus by a minus gives a plus!). The resulting positive numbers are then all added together. The final step, of dividing this sum by the number of cases in order to give us an *average* rather than a *total* figure for dispersion, then gives the total variance.

Standard deviation

This is the most sophisticated and most often used measure of dispersion, yet it is simply the square root of the variance. So if you've understood the notion of the variance, understanding that of the standard deviation should follow fairly easily. As stated above, we need to square all the values in the calculation of the variance in order to eliminate the problem of the minus numbers cancelling out the positive numbers. Well, this final step of calculating standard deviation aims to return the figure of dispersion to the original scale of measurement – and it does this simply by taking its square root. (This is why you will often find the symbols for standard deviation and variance written as SD and SD^2 respectively).

As this book actively tries to avoid the use of numbers, the derivation of standard deviation will not be included here. However, it is a good idea to have an awareness of how we arrived at the figure of standard deviation in order to see the bigger picture – to enable us to better conceptualize how, as a measure of dispersion, it relates to the measure of central tendency (i.e. the mean).

The steps in the calculation of the standard deviation (and thus also the variance) are:

- Measure the deviation (i.e. distance) of each score from the mean.
- Square these deviations in order to rid ourselves of the +/– problem.
- Add these squared deviations to obtain the total deviation figure for the whole sample.
- Divide this by the number of scores (n) to obtain the average for the sample (this is the Variance – SD^2).
- Finally, take the square root of the variance to obtain the Standard Deviation (SD).

2.2.2 Everyday examples

We often encounter ranges – the simplest of the aforementioned measures of dispersion – on a day-to-day basis, probably without even realizing it. Wherever there is some form of consumer choice to be made, for example, there is usually mention of a range – whether this be the range of designer clothing just launched by the latest reality TV celebrity, the price range of pay-as–you-go mobiles, or the range of beer prices at the local pub. We may also get to see the temperature range during the weather forecasts each day, and most people are probably aware of their current position on their salary scale and council tax banding (essentially, both examples of further types of range). Whether concerning finance, temperature or clothing, all of these are measures referring to the distance between the lowest or smallest value to the highest or greatest value.

Standard deviations are much less likely to make their presence felt in everyday situations – yet they do still surface here and there, most notably on 'technical' aspects of various phenomena. Mention of the standard deviation can now and then be spotted toward the end of various news reports, particularly in areas such as finance and education, but also covering topics as diverse as road traffic safety (Seaton 2006), sport (Buckley 2007) and music (Burkeman 2006). In each of these and other cases, the standard deviation is being reported as a more accurate and representative measure of dispersion than the range.

Talking of music sales, if we revisit the music-buying scenario, first introduced in 2.1.2, where we have already discussed the lack of clarity regarding which measure of central tendency was used to make sales claims, we could similarly consider this in terms of the absence of a dispersion figure. In other words, the range – or any other measure of distribution for that matter – of payments being made for the album download was rarely quoted. At least some measure of distribution is needed to accompany the 'typical' payment of £4.00 in order to see the full picture. It could be the case that some buyers could have paid a tenner while others paid a penny – or everyone could have paid between, say, £3.75 and £4.24. Similarly the impact of outliers was not really considered – a few extreme payments of £100.00 could distort the mean considerably (just as we have already seen with the 'politics' example of 2.1.2 and the preferred number of partners controversy of 2.1.3) which could have a dramatic impact on the amount apparently being paid for the album, and thus an impact on the perceived popularity of the 'pay what you like' initiative.

New developments and innovative approaches to the creation and distribution of music, and understanding the success or the impact of these, is important for its consumers as well as for its creators. However, assessing such an impact requires accuracy and, as with many other areas, this needs both an appropriate measure of central tendency and an appropriate measure of dispersion – and a clear statement of which measure is being used (Witte and Witte 2004: 76). It will be interesting to see how this develops as a music selling model over the next few years – or whether, by the time you read this, Spotify on the Iphone will have turned everything around once again! (Keegan 2009).

2.2.3 From the literature

While the range tends to be quoted more often than the standard deviation in every day examples of spread or dispersion, the reverse is often true when it comes to the use of these measures of dispersion in psychological research – and thus their appearance in the literature. The standard deviation is a common feature of most reports of quantitative analysis, but the range is not used to such an extent as it simply offers much less information than either the standard deviation or variance. As mentioned previously while describing the mode and other measures of central tendency, measures of dispersion such as the standard deviation tend to be overshadowed by the results of inferential analyses. However, while there may be less emphasis given to the standard deviation than to inferential results, it is still (almost) always quoted in results sections. Some examples of standard deviation measures from the literature are outlined below, each being used to illustrate the differences between participants in different conditions. In each of the following studies, the different groups are composed of exclusively male or exclusively female participants, with the research being aimed at investigating sex differences, firstly regarding intelligence (both in terms of estimates and actual measures), and then of the emotionality of participants.

The topic of intelligence in psychology is never that far away from controversy, or is at least frequently the subject of a good deal of healthy debate. Such debate can include differences in viewpoints over whether intelligence is mostly inherited or acquired, of whether it can change markedly over time (usually with the emphasis on how it can be increased) or of the very nature of intelligence itself – that is, what it actually means or represents. Even more controversial are aspects such as race or sex differences in measured IQ. One of the many studies which have considered the latter area, that is, whether there are genuine differences in intelligence between men and women, was conducted by Rammstedt and Rammsayer (2000), although the emphasis in this case was slightly different from many other studies in that the focus was on IQ which was *estimated* rather than *measured*.

The Rammstedt and Rammsayer (2000) study was based on approximately equal numbers of male and female students estimating their own IQ scores on each of Thurstone's seven primary mental abilities (Thurstone 1938), and four additional types of intelligence proposed by Gardner (1983). Gender differences were identified for only some of these abilities. Male participants rated their mathematical, logical and spatial intelligence higher than did the female participants, while the females in the study gave higher scores than did the males for musical and interpersonal intelligence. No significant differences were found between male and female estimates for the remaining six abilities.

Interestingly – particularly from our perspective here of considering measures of dispersion – the male and female standard deviations differed much more on the two abilities where the women scored highest than on the three abilities where the men scored highest. For both musical and interpersonal ability there was a much wider distribution of scores for male than for female participants, suggesting that some male participants rated themselves very high and some very low on these abilities, while the scores for the female participants were much more closely distributed around the central mean. In the case of the three abilities where men estimated themselves higher, there appeared to be no such marked difference in the distribution of the male and female scores. As it might be a bit difficult to keep all these results floating around in one's head, they have been summarized in Table 2.1.

Table 2.1 Standard deviations of self-estimates on five ability scales. Adapted from Rammstedt and Rammsayer (2000)

	Male participants	Female participants	Difference in SD
Mathematical ability	12.7	16.4	−3.7
Logical ability	16.0	13.0	3.0
Spatial ability	15.9	14.2	1.7
Musical ability	24.0	16.9	7.1
Interpersonal ability	15.7	8.1	7.6

If only the central tendencies (i.e. the means) of these ability scores had been investigated, then differences in the patterns of scores between males and females for these abilities would not have been noted. In other words, we would not have known that men are much more diverse than women when it comes to reflecting upon and estimating their own level of ability in these areas

A further study investigating male–female differences in intelligence was carried out by Deary et al. (2003), this time using actual measurements of intelligence as opposed to estimates. Their research question was focused on the over-representation of adult males at the upper extremes of ability scales, and they sought to investigate the development of this by re-examining data which was originally recorded seventy years previously as part of the Scottish mental survey of 1932. They found that although there were no significant differences between the boys and girls tested at that time in terms of their *mean* scores, there were significant differences in the *standard deviations* of the scores for boys and girls. They found that the distribution of scores for boys were much wider than that for girls, and that boys were over-represented at both the low and high extremes of the intelligence scales. They suggest that these findings may contribute to our understanding of why there is a slight excess of men over women in the proportions achieving first class university degrees, and why there is also an excess of males with learning difficulties (Deary et al. 2003).

The researchers acknowledge that awareness of such greater variability (i.e. higher standard deviation) of male ability scores is not new, and that as early as the 1950s this was being used as an explanation for patterns of achievement among university students, with the suggestion by Watts (1953) of a link between the difference in IQ variability of men and women and the tendency for men to gain more first and third class – but fewer second class – degrees than women.

For our purposes of considering the use of the standard deviation, this study is useful as it shows that, had just the means been calculated (i.e. descriptive statistics based only on the central tendency value) then no differences between the ability levels of the boys and girls would have been observed because the means themselves were not significantly different. It is only when one is considering the nature and extent of the dispersion of scores that the difference between the boys and girls can be detected, thus allowing the authors to posit the possible connections between different patterns of dispersion and the over-representation of men at the learning difficulties and first class hons ends of the cognitive ability spectrum.

A study conducted by Brebner (2003) continues this theme of looking at the psychological differences between men and women (there do seem to be lots of these!), but this time with the focus on emotion rather than intelligence. Using the self-report data from a sample of Australian students, the researchers determined the frequency with which participants experienced eight separate emotions. They found that male and female participants differed in their experience of three of these emotions; *affection* and *sadness* in the case of women, and *pride* in the case of men. However, in this study there appeared to be no sex difference in the magnitude of the standard deviations – the standard deviation of the male emotion scores did not differ from that of the female participants. This is in direct contrast to the expectations of the researchers, who predicted that women's standard deviation on the emotionality scales should be larger than that of men's. The researchers suggest that the findings reflect a weakening of traditional sex roles and stereotyping among Australian students and that the perception of gender differences in emotional expression are exaggerated by stereotyping. For our, more methodologically based perspective, the study again shows the desirability of examining measures both of dispersion and central tendency. In this case, had only the former (i.e. the spread of scores) been considered then the differences would not have been noted This is in direct contrast to that of the previous Deary et al. (2003) study, where differences in standard deviations were found, but differences in means were not.

2.2.4 Narrative

If we apply the areas which we have covered above to the ongoing developments in our hypothetical reaction time experiments, we should now be able to add a little more weight to the central tendency results we have already considered. As Table 2.2 shows, in the case of the data collected from the first week and the last three weeks of the experiment, we would use the standard deviation as the preferred measure of dispersion as this best reflects the nature of the data which had been collected, that is, on a scale level of measurement. In the case of the data collected from Week 2, we would most likely use the range or interquartile range in place of the standard deviation as this would be a more suitable measure of dispersion for data of an ordinal level. Note that the space indicating the preferred measure of dispersion for the nominal data collected during Week 3 has been left blank. This is because, due to the very limited nature of the nominal level of measurement, it is not normally possible to use a measure of dispersion such as those mentioned above to describe the pattern of distribution of these data.

As we can see, this research on Friday morning alertness is now beginning to build into a nice little project, with the researcher approaching the topic from a number of angles, at least in terms of the levels of measurement and initial descriptive analyses. Before commencement of inferential analyses, though, he comes to the decision that the project actually needs to be extended in order to provide additional perspectives on this Friday morning feeling. He therefore sets out to build upon the above via the inclusion of a number of additional measures (these being

Table 2.2 Aspects of the reaction time study in terms of research design and levels of measurement

Week	Investigation	Design	Level of measurement	Distribution	Central tendency	Spread
1	Experiment	Between	Scale	Continuous	Mean	SD
2	Experiment	Between	Ordinal	Discrete	Median	Range/IQR
3	Experiment	Between	Nominal	Discrete	Mode	
4	Experiment	Within	Scale	Continuous	Mean	SD
5	Experiment	Within	Scale	Continuous	Mean	SD
6	Non-experiment	Within	Scale	Continuous	Mean	SD

described in 2.3.4, featured as part of our treatment of standard scores).

2.2.5 Further reading

Field, A. P. (2005). *Discovering Statistics Using SPSS (and Sex, Drugs and Rock 'n' Roll) 2nd Edition*. Sage. section 1.5.

Holt, N. and Walker, I. (2009). *Research with people: Theory, Plans and Practicals*. Palgrave Macmillan. chapter 3.

Howitt, D. and Cramer, D. (2008). *Introduction to SPSS in Psychology 4th Edition*. Pearson Prentice Hall. chapter 5.

Howitt, D. and Cramer, D. (2008). *Introduction to Statistics in Psychology 4th Edition*. Pearson Prentice Hall. chapter 5.

Miles, J. and Banyard, P. (2007). *Understanding and Using Statistics in Psychology*. London: Sage. chapter 2.

2.3 Summarizing findings via percentiles and standard scores

2.3.1 Concepts

So far in this chapter we have considered approaches to summarizing data, or of summarizing the scores in a dataset, via measures of central tendency and dispersion. This summarizing of scores has thus far dealt with raw scores, that is, the actual measurements on the dependent variable which are recorded by researchers, whether this be in the form of continuous data such as reaction times, ranked data such as the first, second or third participant to complete a task, or simple counts of participants in various, mutually exclusive categories.

However, raw scores alone often do not tell the whole story, and knowledge of an individual score in a given dataset is not always helpful unless we have some knowledge of the other scores in the dataset too. In other words, in order to fully interpret a given test score or result, we really need to know not just the score or the rank, but also some information about *other* scores within the class or the group. We therefore need to be able to *compare* a given score with the scores for a 'norm' group. There are two common ways of doing this in psychological research, the first via the calculation of percentiles, the second via the production of Z-scores. (There are actually further approaches to standardizing scores, but these tend to be much less frequent than percentiles or Z-scores. However, one such approach, the T-score, does turn up from time to time and is thus covered briefly in the box at the end of the section.)

Percentiles

These are the conceptually simplest measures used to emphasize relative, as opposed to absolute or raw scores. They show the relative position of a score, indicating the position of that score (or the participant attaining that score) by specifying the percentage of the group below that score. Or, more accurately, by stating the percentage of the group *below* that score, plus half the percent right *at* that score. We have already encountered the percentile, albeit indirectly, in the section on measures of central tendency and dispersion. In terms of central tendency, the median is simply a particular instance of a percentile – it is always the 50th percentile of a given set of scores. Similarly in terms of spread or dispersion of scores, the interquartile range is essentially just the distance between the 25th and 75th percentiles.

Z-scores

These follow on directly from standard deviation, as the Z-score is a measure of how far a given score differs from the average score, as measured in *standard deviation units*. That may sound a little complex, but all it really means is that the Z-score is a measure of how far a given score is from the mean score – of how far away, say, *our* exam result or reaction time is from the most *typical* exam result or reaction time. It is calculated by working out the difference between the given score and the mean, and then dividing this figure by the standard deviation. This is actually a relatively simple process to complete by hand, in the event of a desperate need to calculate a Z-score whenever a computer is unavailable – but probably the most important thing to remember when you see a Z-score is that it is simply telling us how far a particular score differs from the mean score, and that the larger the value of a Z-score, the further away that score is from the mean.

2.3.2 Everyday examples

Let's take a simple numerical example here to show how percentiles are actually derived by considering these two sets of ten raw scores: 1,2,3,4,5,5,6,7,8,9 and 4,5,5,5,5,5,5,5,5,10 (unfortunately, this is one of those few occasions within the book where looking at numbers is actually unavoidable). We could think of these figures as being the number of words correctly spelled by ten school children on two spelling tests.

Now, if someone attained a raw score of 5 on the first test, what percentile score would this represent? Well, remember that the percentile of a group of numbers or scores is derived by taking the percentage below that score and then adding half of the percentage right at that score. So, a score of 5 would be at the 50th percentile, as 40% of the scores are below 5, and 20% of scores are actually at 5. If we add the 40% to half of the 20% (i.e. 10%) we end up with 40+10=50. It's that easy! If we consider the results of the second fictitious spelling test, then we can see that the score of 5 is once again at the 50th percentile, as 10% of the scores are below 5, and 80% are actually at 5, so adding the 10 to 40 (i.e. half of 80%) we again reach a percentile figure of 50.

If we consider the raw score of 4 on the above tests, however, things are a little different. This would represent a percentile of 35 for the first dataset (as 30% of the scores are below 4, and 10% of the scores are at 4), but would represent a percentile of just 5 for the second set of scores (as in this case 0% of the scores are below 4, and just 10% are at that score). A child taking these two spelling tests and scoring four correct answers each time, therefore, would actually be doing relatively much better on the first test than the second, even though the number of correct answers he or she obtained would be exactly the same.

In terms of everyday application, percentiles are often used by personnel departments or human resources for purposes of development. Candidates for promotion, for example, may undergo aptitude tests for the potential new job, with the results of these scores being converted to percentiles so that the promotion board doesn't just have the raw aptitude score, but also knows where this score is positioned in terms of all the other candidates (and sometimes in relation to a much wider 'norm group' of scores).

Percentiles, then, are fairly straightforward, although there are a few points to remember when dealing with them. The first being not to confuse them with percentages – if a student scores 80% in an exam this may seem very high, but if most people earned marks above this, then that students' percentile score may be very low – remember, it is all about comparison. The second point to note is that percentiles are not equal units of measurement. For instance, the meaning or interpretation of a difference of five percentile points between the exam scores of two students will depend on the position on the percentile scale where this difference is to be found. Percentile scales tends to exaggerate differences near the mean and collapse differences at the extremes, so this difference of five points may actually be more salient if it were positioned between 50 and 60 than if it were to be found between 80 and 90. Lastly it should also be noted that, because of this lack of equidistance, percentiles cannot be averaged nor treated in any other arithmetic or mathematical way.

The Z-score is a little more sophisticated than the percentile, and because of this is usually the preferred type of standard score (in fact, it is actually usually referred to as 'the' standard score). Working out a Z-score requires that we already know the mean and standard deviation of a set of scores, and that we are willing to do a little arithmetic – although not too much! For example, if we have calculated that the standard deviation of a set of scores is 6, then we know that a raw score which is 6 above the mean score is one 'unit' of standard deviation above the mean. In other words, in this case a raw score of 6 would have a Z-score of 1. If our given raw score is 12 above the mean score then this is placed at two units of standard deviation above the mean, and therefore has a Z-score of 2. Similarly, raw scores of 3, 6 and 9 would have Z-scores of 0.5, 1 and 1.5 respectively.

Z-scores are often used in order that we may compare scores or results that would not normally be comparable, such as scores recorded via different levels of measurement. This is because the Z-score is a 'dimensionless quantity', that is, regardless of what is actually being measured in a psychological investigation, be it reaction times after drinking a particular type of coffee or attitudes toward that coffee after viewing its latest trendy TV adverts, the Z-score is only concerned with how far a given score is from the mean. Thus it can not be expressed in terms of the quantities being measured but only in terms of the standard units of distance of a given score from a mean score. It is therefore considered dimensionless in that it has no units of its own, and is thus just a pure number.

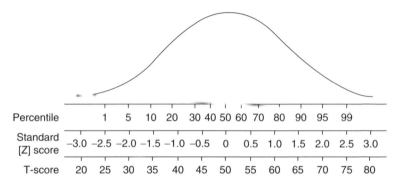

Percentile		1	5	10	20	30	40	50	60	70	80		90	95	99
Standard [Z] score	−3.0	−2.5	−2.0		−1.5	−1.0	−0.5	0	0.5	1.0	1.5	2.0	2.5		3.0
T-score	20	25	30	35		40	45	50	55	60	65	70		75	80

Figure 2.1 Relationship between percentiles, Z-scores and T-scores

The relationship of Z-scores to other standardized measures is illustrated in Figure 2.1. It may also be worth noting that Z-scores have the following properties:

- The mean of a set of Z-scores always equals 0.
- The standard deviation of a set of Z-scores always equals 1.
- The distribution of a set of Z-scores is identical to that of the raw scores from which they were derived.

All this talk of standardizing scores may at first simply appear to complicate matters (the cynical among us may think that it could be simply a case of more stats for its own sake!) but the standard score is actually very useful in three respects. Firstly, it gives us a relative as well as an absolute value of a given score; secondly, it allows us to deal with scores which have been measured on different types of scales; and thirdly, it enables us to minimize the distortive effects of extreme scores. We'll cover the second and third points in Section 2.3.3., but for an illustration of the first point, see the scenario (adapted from Krantzer 2007) below:

Boy: Mum! I got 88 on my statistics test today!
Mother: That's very good son. You must be very happy!
Boy: Uhh ... yes, but it was 88 out of a possible 200.
Mother: Oh! I'm sorry. I guess you didn't do too well then.
Boy: But I got the third highest score in the class.
Mother: Yay! Very Good!

Boy: Uh ... yes, but there are only three of us actually in that class ...
Mother: ......?

This helps to illustrate the first of the aforementioned reasons for using standard scores – to avoid the limitations of raw scores or even ranked scores. As previously mentioned above, these alone often do not tell the whole story, such as in the case of the raw score of 88 and the rank score of 3 in the scenario above. Here, knowing the raw score on the test on a scale level of measurement doesn't help that much unless we know the potential maximum (and minimum?) of the entire range, or other measure of dispersion. Similarly, knowing the position of that student on an ordinal level of measurement also doesn't help much without knowing how many other scores are being ranked (i.e. the size of the cohort). However, if these were converted to Z-scores, we would be able to immediately gauge the relative impact of that score of 88!

Hopefully the above examples should help to emphasize one of the main aspects of standard scores – that it's all relative. The absolute score of 4 in the spelling test example represents a quite different level of achievement depending on the test in which it was achieved – it represents a relatively higher achievement on the first than the second. Similarly, the score of 88 above could be considered for either a commendation or condemnation by the boy's mum depending on one's perspective and on the scores of everyone else in the class. Let's see how these have been used in a few actual studies...

2.3.3 From the literature

One of the really useful applications of the standard score is that it allows us to more easily compare scores from different kinds of distributions. In other words it allows us to compare and to combine scores measured in many different ways. Consider this scenario (taken from Howitt and Cramer 2008c: 46), which describes a research student's approach to assessing the level of commitment which parents display in supporting their children's sporting activities, and the potential effects which this commitment level may have on the psychological well-being of the child. Rather than simply asking parents to rate themselves on how much they felt that they were committed or involved with their child's sport (the sport in this particular case being tennis), parents were asked to indicate this commitment through a number of different channels, such as how much money they spent supporting their child's activities, for example on coaching, equipment and also clothing. They were also asked to indicate the distance they travelled, or were prepared to travel, to tennis training sessions, matches or other events. Other aspects relating to their sporting commitment were also considered, including the number of hours per week they spent watching their child play tennis, a count of the actual number of tournaments the child had attended and so on.

As you can see, this resulted in a considerable variety of data, including measurements of financial expenditure, distance travelled, number of attendances and various amounts of time. These also represent very different levels of measurement. As these various measurements are so diverse it would be difficult to analyse them via the usual methods, for example, of adding or averaging etc., as they represent quite different concepts. However, if the researchers converted all the various raw scores to Z-scores then they would be able to obtain an overall 'commitment' figure. As Z-scores are dimensionless quantities, they can easily be added or subtracted regardless of the original scales of measurement. In the above case, Z-scores derived from raw scores of the diverse measurements of time, money and frequency can indeed be added together to provide an overall figure.

This use of the standard score to provide an overall, dimensionless measure when faced with data collected from diverse scales or sources is often to be found in the literature. For example, a study aimed at exploring ways in which teenagers could be encouraged to engage in a healthier lifestyle investigated the relationship between motivation, self-worth, self-esteem and physical activity. As these variables were measured along different scales and levels of measurement, the researchers converted the raw scores into Z-scores to enable more effective manipulation and analysis of the collected data (Biddle and Wang 2003).

Similarly, with a recent study investigating the development of children's literacy ability, the researcher made use of Z-scores in order to effectively deal with a variety of different types of measurement (Korat 2009). This investigation focused upon the effect of infant–maternal interaction in the form of maternal 'teaching talk', and how this can be influenced by the mother's own educational and literacy levels during various observed activities. The dependent variable of emergent literacy was assessed via six different scales of differing magnitude and levels of measurement, including print concept, phonological awareness, receptive vocabulary and word recognition. The researcher standardized the scores attained on each of these scales in order that these could be combined into a single overall 'emergent literacy' score. This greatly simplified analysis and enabled the researchers to uncover support for the positive relationship between maternal and infant literacy levels as regards the mother's use of 'teaching talk'.

The above has hopefully gone some way to clarifying the use of the Z-score for helping to deal with diverse forms of data in psychological research. One further illustration, based on the increasingly familiar investigation into Friday morning alertness, is described below.

2.3.4 Narrative

We can use our ongoing reaction time scenario to illustrate the use of Z-scores if we consider an extension of the investigation to incorporate a few further measures. Let us imagine that, after a few weeks of the aforementioned reaction time studies, it begins to dawn on the researcher that he has actually been rather narrow in his focus, and that paying too much attention to the performance of the participants on his computer program may actually detract from the wider issue of post-Thursday alertness with which he is so concerned – in other words, that determining the reaction time of students may not be the *only* way of establishing their Friday morning mental fitness.

So he decides to expand the investigation by incorporating three additional measures of alertness into the research, these being comprised of a task-completion exercise where participants are required to solve a number of algebraic problems within a set time period, and also two self-report questionnaires specifically designed to determine a participant's level of alertness (see for example the ZOGIM-A and THAT questionnaires developed by Shapiro et al. (2006)). The participant's scores on these three additional measures are thus comprised of the number of problems correctly solved within the set time period, and also the ratings derived from the two questionnaires. In the case of the Shapiro et al. instrument, this would take the form of a 10-item self-report index designed on a 6-point scale for THAT, and a 10-item self-report index based on a 5-point scale for ZOGIM-A.

The researcher therefore now as four separate measures with which to gauge the alertness of the students, comprising measurement levels of (1) scale-continuous, the reaction time in milliseconds, (2) scale-discrete, the number of correct task solutions (3) ordinal on a 5-point scale and (4) ordinal on a 6-point scale.

Performing analytical operations on these four measures in order to obtain an overall index of alertness would immediately run into difficulties if they remained in their raw form, that is, it would not be possible to obtain a total value for student alertness by simply adding the recorded reaction time to the ratings given on ZOGIM-A, or by adding the ratings on THAT to the number of problems correctly solved in the algebraic exercise. However, by taking the standard scores approach, the researcher would be able to transform all the raw scores of all the student participants into Z-scores. By then combining these transformed scores, the researcher would be able to establish an overall 'alertness index' for each group of students, that is, the clubbers and the non-clubbers, and then perhaps seek to establish any differences between these in order to establish the effect of hitting the town on a Thursday. An example of the raw and standard scores for one of these participants, along with the calculated alertness index, is illustrated in Table 2.3.

Table 2.3 Addition of Z-scores on individual variables into an 'alertness index'

	Reaction time	Tasks solved	THAT	ZOGIM-A	Alertness index
Levels of measurement	Scale	Scale	Ordinal	Ordinal	
Raw score	320 ms	6 Correct	Medium (3)	Medium (3)	N/A
Z-score	−0.8	1.1	−0.2	0.7	0.8

2.3.5 Further reading

Field, A. P. (2005). *Discovering Statistics Using SPSS (and Sex, Drugs and Rock 'n' Roll) 2nd Edition.* Sage. section 1.53.

Howitt, D. and Cramer, D. (2008). *Introduction to Statistics in Psychology 4th Edition.* Pearson Prentice Hall. chapter 5.

Miles, J. and Banyard, P. (2007). *Understanding and Using Statistics in Psychology.* London: Sage. chapter 3.

One more thing... a note on Z-scores and T-Scores

A less often used, but still important form of standardized score is the T-score. This is based on the Z-score, but with a simple arithmetic operation to remove the minus numbers and decimal points. The formula for creating T-scores is T = 10 (Z) +50 (although you will probably not need to use this). Once trans-formed, T-scores can be added or subtracted more simply than Z-scores due to the absence of minus numbers. Again, prob-ably the most important thing to remember about the T-score is that it is simply telling us how far away any given score is from the mean. The relationship between percentiles, Z-scores and T-scores (as used in this case in educational psychology) is illustrated in Figure 2.1.

2.4 Summary

In introducing the fundamentals of descriptive data analysis, this chapter has covered what has probably been relatively familiar ground to many, such as the common sense notions of the average and range, as well as a few areas which you may well have seen for the very first time, for example, Z-scores, variance and standard deviation. Regardless of previous familiarity, though, the approach taken here should have helped the level one psychology student to see how to summarize data (for summarizing is indeed the primary purpose of descriptive statistics) in three ways: by providing a typical score of a given dataset, by indicating the variations of scores within that data set and finally by indicating how a given score relates to all other scores in that dataset.

Each of these perspectives on descriptive data analysis reflects considerations made in the first chapter, that is, that in order to conduct appropriate descriptive analysis we must first be aware of the nature of the variables we are trying to analyse. In the case of the first of these three perspectives, we should ensure that our calculation of a typical score, or *measure of central tendency*, should be appropriate for the level of measurement. In the case of a nominal level of measurement this should be the mode, in the case of ordinal this should be either the mode or (most likely) the median, while in the case of scale this could be the mode, the median or (most probably) the mean. Similarly, our calculations of the appropriate *measure of dispersion* should also reflect the particular level of measurement, with the interquartile range being well suited to data of an ordinal level of measurement and the standard deviation being the dispersion measure of choice for the equidistant points on a scale level of measurement.

The approaches we use to convert raw scores to percentiles or standard scores – our third *standardization* perspective on the provision of summary descriptive statistics – also relates to the concepts of Chapter 1, as such approaches tend to transform our original data into that which can be considered to be of a scale level of measurement. Furthermore, the areas of percentiles and (particularly) Z-scores also build on the concepts introduced in this chapter – more specifically the way in which the mean and standard deviation can be used to produce dimensionless, standard scores which are applicable to any dependent variable being measured, and which can be added, subtracted and generally manipulated in ways that raw scores often cannot.

These aspects of descriptive statistics can sometimes be considered as an end in themselves, as particular investigations may only require that the collected data be summarized via the production of, for example, means, standard deviations and Z-scores. It is more usually the case, however, that descriptive statistics represent just the first wave of analysis, to be undertaken in order to summarize the initial findings prior to any further inferential analysis being performed on the data. The techniques of these inferential analyses will be detailed in Chapter 4 of this book, following coverage of the essential 'preparation' for such analyses in Chapter 3 ...

1. What is an outlier?

   a. A set of data outside the data file.
   b. A single score that is very different form the others.
   c. A score derived from a participant who has lied.
   d. A variable that cannot be quantified.

2. Which of the following is most affected by outliers?

   a. The mode.
   b. The mean.
   c. The median.
   d. They are all equally affected.

3. The standard deviation is the square root of the:

   a. Coefficient of determination.
   b. Sum of squares.
   c. Variance.
   d. Range.

4. Which of the following is true?

   a. The variance is a measure of dispersion and is the square root of the standard deviation.
   b. The variance is a measure of dispersion and is the square of the standard deviation.
   c. The variance is a measure of dispersion which has no relation to the standard deviation.
   d. The standard deviation is the square of the variance.

5. The interquartile range:

   a. Is always larger than the range.
   b. Is another way of referring to the range.

c. Nine times out of ten is identical to the mean.

d. Is usually smaller than the range.

6. Which of the following is NOT a feature of descriptive statistics?

   a. Descriptive statistics organize and summarize data.

   b. Descriptive statistics describe patterns in the data.

   c. Descriptive statistics inform us of the nature of significant relationships between variables.

   d. Descriptive statistics include measures such as the mean, mode and median.

7. If a distribution is multimodal, what does this mean?

   a. It will not be a normal distribution.

   b. The data has been entered incorrectly.

   c. It will be a normal distribution.

   d. It will have to be checked with a Levene's test.

8. Which of the following is a good measure of the spread of scores?

   a. Mean.

   b. Mode.

   c. Median.

   d. None of the above.

9. Which of the following is true?

   a. Variance can be calculated for any sort of data.

   b. Variance is a standard formula to indicate the variability of all scores for a particular variable.

   c. Variance cannot be calculated for score data.

   d. Variance and the median are very similar.

10. Dispersion is to central tendency as variance is to:

    a. Standard deviation.

    b. Range.

    c. Mean.

    d. Z-score.

3 **Prelude to testing**

We have thus far considered the fundamentals of quantitative data analysis both in terms of the essential concepts, for example, levels of measurement and design, and the basics of descriptive statistics. The next logical step would thus seem to be the progression to the more complex material, that is to inferential analysis...

However, moving too abruptly into this area can sometimes lead to various problems, as students (and some text books) can often neglect the 'prerequisites' of inferential analysis – of establishing the 'why' and the 'when' of their use. It is often the case that student assignments involving inferential statistics tend to lose marks not because of a lack of understanding of the statistical tests themselves, but of the circumstances within which they should be applied. Some classic examples of this include the within–between confusion, that is, when students mistakenly apply *between groups* testing to data which is of a *within groups* design. Another old chestnut is using parametric tests in order to analyse non-parametric data due to student confusion over scale and ordinal levels of measurement. These are simple enough mistakes in a way, and are really just oversights which we've probably all made at one time or another, but they are also simple enough to avoid with a little bit of thought and preparation. Hence the inclusion of this chapter!

This third chapter is therefore aimed at outlining the steps which need to be taken, or at least considered, in order to increase the likelihood of choosing the most appropriate test when performing inferential data analyses. It seeks to do this by providing a grounding in areas such as samples and populations, and also by considering the phrasing of research questions as explicit hypotheses. Further, it outlines the checks which we should carry out before applying parametric tests to our data – that is, it covers the requirements which must be met in order for parametric statistics to be used effectively.

As such, this chapter aims to form a bridge between Chapters 2 and 4 (hence its position as Chapter 3!), or more seriously, to ease the transition from descriptive statistics to inferential statistics so that when we *do* get there it should all fall nicely into place...

Due to this 'bridge' aspect, it is also structured slightly differently than the other chapters of the book, with less emphasis on analogies and examples from the literature. Indeed, it is usually the case that research studies do not report the pretesting of data to ensure that parametric assumptions are met, due to the emphasis placed on the actual results themselves – hence the streamlining of these sections in this particular chapter.

Populations, samples and standard errors

3.1.1 Concepts

Psychologists are a rather varied bunch, largely by virtue of the varied nature of the discipline, but they do share a certain common interest. That is most tend to be interested in the behaviour of people in general, or at least of large numbers of people – or at least of large numbers of certain *types* of people. As a result, many of us endeavour to engage in research of various kinds with the aim of producing findings which are applicable to these large numbers of people.

However, the opportunities to study such numbers directly are extremely rare – unheard of, even. Rather than to study a whole population of interest directly, which could involve surveying perhaps a million people, researchers will instead conduct their investigations with a much smaller number of individuals and then seek to apply the results of these investigations to the larger population. This is not simply a case, however, of studying a few dozen participants and then expecting (or just hoping?) that the study's results can be used to describe hundreds, thousands or even millions of others. Rather than to simply hope for the best, researchers make effective use of sophisticated sampling procedures and use these side by side with inferential statistics. This then enables the said researchers to infer, with a relatively high degree of accuracy, the characteristics of a given population from the characteristics of a representative sample. In other words, we *infer* one (population) from the other (sample) – this giving rise to the term *infer*ential statistics.

So, instead of undertaking research with relatively large numbers of people, we will most often undertake our investigation with a relatively small *sample* of the population of interest, and then generalize the results to the larger population. This is certainly the case on a large-scale study such as a national survey, but even on a smaller scale, samples will usually be used rather than entire populations due to considerations of time and cost. The most important thing to note here is that our sample should be *representative* of the population of interest to enable us to generalize in this way.

However, in reality there is no such thing as a perfectly representative sample. No matter how hard we try to ensure that our sample is representative, there will always be a degree of difference between the figures we have for a given study conducted with a sample and the 'true' figures which would have been derived had we been able to access the entire population. For example, calculating the mean age of a cohort of a hundred psychology students based on a 10% sample may give us a mean very close to that of the whole cohort, but probably not exactly the same. So, how would we resolve this? Well, still using this student cohort as an example of our population of interest, we may be able to simply increase the size of the sample – as the closer the match between the size of the sample and that of the actual population becomes, the closer too will be the match between their respective means. In a case such as this, we may even be able to access the whole population, as the population itself only comprises a hundred individuals. This approach soon runs into problems with larger populations though – for example, in the case of calculating the mean age of the entire university, or even more problematically, of calculating the mean age of all the students in the UK.

A more realistic and practical approach to dealing with this would be to use multiple samples. In the case of the example above, lets say that we take not only a single 10% sample and calculate the mean age, but also that we also take a further 10% sample and repeat the process. We could then incorporate the results from these two samples by taking the average of both (i.e. by calculating the mean of the two sample means). Indeed, we could adopt this approach with a third, fourth or even fifth sample, each one being randomly drawn from the 'pool' of the population – be this composed of a hundred students or a thousand – with the idea here being that the greater number of samples we use, the closer our average sample mean will be to the true population mean.

This is where we use the notion of the standard error of the mean – sometimes also known as just 'standard error'. The standard error concerns the extent to which the means across all our samples differ. It is therefore a measure of how the mean for the population differs from sample to sample. More technically, it is essentially the standard deviation of the means of all the samples used.

Many students find this a difficult to concept to grasp initially, and it is sometimes better to describe this concept via example (as in Section 3.1.2) and analogy (as in Table 3.1). Table 3.1. is based on a number of parallels to the concepts we have already covered in the previous chapter, so hopefully as long as you have already got a grasp of concepts such as mean score, standard deviation and the normal distribution, it shouldn't be too much of a leap to extend this to the concepts of mean of means, standard error, and the sampling distribution of the mean.

The analogy of Table 3.1 usually eases the conceptualization process, but only if the concepts introduced in the previous chapter have been fully understood. The statistics modules of psychology degrees do tend to include many more 'step-by-step' aspects than other modules, and this is a classic instance of such a step-by-step approach, that is, in this case to understand standard error one really does need to get a good handle on standard deviation. So, if you are still unclear about standard deviation, it is well worth revisiting the previous chapter before reading further.

Table 3.1 Comparison between concepts based on means, and concepts based on *mean* of means

If we conceptualize	Then we can consider
The *mean score* as being the mid point in a *normal distribution of scores*	The *mean of sample means* as being the mid point in a normal distribution of sample means (the *sampling distribution of the mean*).
The *standard deviation* of a normal distribution of scores as being a measure of how much the scores on average deviate from this mean	The *standard error of the mean* of a normal distribution of sample means as being a measure of how much the sample means on average deviate from the population mean.
The smaller the *standard deviation* of a set of *scores*, the more each score is representative of the mean	The smaller the *standard error* of a set of *sample* means, the more each sample is representative of the population.

3.1.2 Examples and illustrations

As an illustration of the importance of the above, let's consider the area of academic performance. We frequently hear of new research findings demonstrating links between students' academic performance and factors such as diet, stress or fatigue (or even staying out late on Thursdays). Much of this research tends to focus on the physiological bases of performance – for example, the impact of blood sugar levels on concentration among students who skip breakfast – and tends to be reported quite often in the popular media (and appropriately enough quite often on breakfast news). A review of such studies can be found in Pollitt (1995). Almost all such research relies on sampling. For example, if we wished to determine the effects that missing breakfast has on a target population of 11-year old UK school children, that is, those in year six of the UK school system, then our population would be comprised of hundreds of thousands of scores – and maybe tens of thousands of individual children. Directly studying the breakfast eating and performance levels of *every* 11-year old would clearly be virtually impossible. Therefore a sample of 11-year olds would be selected for the study; the sample being selected in order to be representative of the population from which it was taken in order that generalization is able to take place.

There are various ways of ensuring the degree to which a sample can be considered as being representative of the population; randomized, stratified, multistaged, and clustered sampling techniques to name but a few (see Fu et al. 2007 for a study of investigating the links between nutrition and school performance which has incorporated most of these approaches). However, the emphasis here is on the use of the standard error in research rather than sampling methodology. With studies such as the above, the standard error would need to be calculated and reported in order for the reader to interpret how well the sample actually did represent the population – the smaller the standard error, the more representative the sample would be of the population. Indeed, in the Fu et al. (2007) study, a relatively large standard error is recorded, and is cited as a reason for repeating the study using larger samples, that is, because larger standard errors imply that samples are less representative of populations, and the use of larger samples is a way of potentially reducing the size of this standard error.

The use of the standard error in this way is not restricted to studies which have obtained samples from relatively large populations, such as all 11-year old schoolchildren in the UK, but also to where the research is on a much smaller scale with a population of a hundred or so rather than one of several hundred thousand. Actually, a scenario involving samples from a relatively small population may be the preferred way of explaining this...

Let's say we were interested in the activities of a particular student cohort – the current year one of the psychology degree, for example – and that we were interested *only* in this cohort. In other words, we would have no interest in the students of other courses or of other years or of generalizing our findings to students at other universities. Our attention is focused purely on this first year psychology class of, say, two hundred students – this would therefore be our target population. In keeping with several of the scenarios used earlier in this book, the activity of interest in this hypothetical example is the time spent socializing each evening in the union bar. So how could we approach this?

Well, in this case and with such a small population, we could feasibly approach each of the two hundred students individually and ask them. It may well be time-consuming and tedious, but we would get there in the end (unlike in the all-UK school example above). So let's say we did actually approach *every* student on a cohort with the question of how many hours on average per week each one spends in the union bar, and we find that the average for the whole cohort is ten hours. That's the result we were looking for – the population mean – but the method of deriving it – by individually asking two hundred people – was not particularly desirable, being very inefficient.

A much more resource-efficient way of attaining the population mean would be to take the multiple samples approach, for example, to randomly draw samples of say five students and to calculate the sample mean (of hours in the bar) of each of these samples of five. What sort of results would we be likely to obtain? Well, the mean of the first sample would probably *not* be exactly ten hours, but most likely be something *close* to it. The mean for our second sample would again probably be close to the population mean. The mean of the third sample might again be close, or even spot on, while the fourth sample mean may be way out, and so on. However many samples we took, the answers could vary considerably but we would expect most to be very close to the population mean, many of them to be quite close, some to be a long way off, and a few to be exactly the same. If we were to plot a graph of these sample means, it might look something like that of Figure 3.1.

Figure 3.1 represents the spread of the means of each of the samples taken – in other words the sampling distribution of the mean. It is a symmetrical distribution and appears to approximate the standard normal distribution, which we will cover in more detail in Section 3.3.

For now, the above may be used to illustrate the notion of standard error – that it is essentially a measure of dispersion, just like the standard deviation we encountered in Section 2.2, and that just as with standard deviation, the greater the value, the greater the variation around the mean. In other words, whereas a large standard deviation refers to a wide dispersion of raw scores around the mean score, a large standard error of the mean refers to a wide

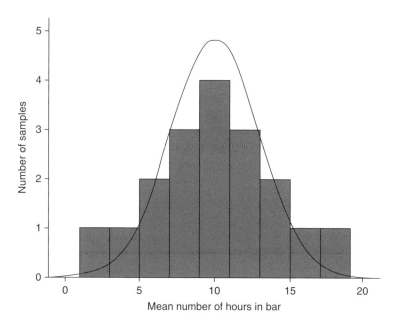

Figure 3.1 Spread of sample means approximating to a normal distribution

dispersion of mean sample scores around the mean of the mean sample scores. Basically, then, the smaller the standard error, the more certain we can be that our sample is representative of the population from which it is drawn.

3.1.3 Further reading

Holt, N. and Walker, I. (2009). *Research with People: Theory, Plans and Practicals*. Palgrave Macmillan. chapter 2.

Howitt, D. and Cramer, D. (2008). *Introduction to Statistics in Psychology 4th Edition*. Pearson Prentice Hall. chapters 9 and 11.

Howitt, D. and Cramer, D. (2008). *Introduction to SPSS in Psychology 4th Edition*. Pearson Prentice Hall. chapters 9 and 12.

3.2 Hypothesis testing, probability and statistical significance

3.2.1 Concepts

When we conduct research in psychology we usually make a prediction of some sort, known more formally as a hypothesis. Such hypotheses are of two basic types – the null and the experimental. The null hypothesis simply states that we expect there to be no statistically significant effect found in our research results, that is, no statistically significant difference or similarity will be found. The experimental hypothesis, in contrast, states that a statistically significant effect *will* be found.

The experimental hypothesis can be stated in one of two ways, either directional (i.e. predicting the direction or nature of the effect) or non-directional (a prediction that there will be an effect, but not of how this effect will be manifested or the direction in which it will occur). It is worth noting that these terms, directional and non-directional, are often interchanged with terms describing the types of tests used to analyse data in accordance with these hypotheses, that is, that directional and non-directional hypotheses may also be referred to as 1-tailed and 2-tailed hypotheses respectively.

Thinking back to our breakfast example above as a potential illustration of these hypotheses, a prediction that skipping breakfast will affect our mid-morning powers of concentration would represent a non-directional hypothesis, whereas a prediction that skipping breakfast will have a *detrimental* effect on such concentration would be considered to be directional hypothesis. A prediction that skipping breakfast would have no effect on our concentration levels whatsoever would thus be a null hypothesis.

Closely associated with the concepts of the null and experimental hypotheses are the notions of probability and statistical significance, which are essential in our interpretation of research results. Of these, the notion of probability is (probably!) the most generally understood. Probability refers to the chance likelihood that a particular result will be seen, or how likely it is that a predicted effect will take place. It is expressed in terms of the ratio of a particular outcome to all possible outcomes. For example, the probability of a coin landing 'heads up' is one divided by two – that is, the particular outcome of the 'heads' side being divided by all possible outcomes of both sides. This is normally expressed as 0.5, or 50%. Similarly, the probability of a dice landing on number six, or on any other number for that matter, is one divided by six (i.e. the particular side being predicted divided by the six sides that are possible). This would therefore be expressed as 0.17, or 17%. The chance of rolling a six on a dice is therefore much less than that of flipping a heads up coin; 0.17 for the dice as opposed to 0.5 for the coin.

The third term here, that of statistical significance, has something of a special meaning in research terms when used to refer to results. Rather than refer to something which is significant in the sense that it is interesting or important, it refers to the result of a research investigation which is likely to have occurred for reasons other than pure chance. An important part of this last sentence is the word 'likely' – statistical significance only tells us that a result or effect is *likely* to have occurred for reasons other than chance factors. It cannot tell us anything more than this, and it certainly cannot *prove* anything. The term 'prove' is generally frowned upon in psychological research, and along with a few other terms (such as 'fact') is generally best avoided! It is also worth noting that the phrase 'statistical significance' rather than simply 'significance' is often used in the literature in order to avoid possible confusion between a result which is statistically significant, and one which is simply significant to the research question. The latter may refer to the findings being significant in the sense of them being noteworthy, interesting or important, but not necessarily that the results are significant in terms of the former, statistical sense.

These three concepts of hypotheses, probability and statistical significance, are used throughout psychological research to enable researchers to make sense of their data analyses and to interpret their findings. Along with an understanding of the relationship between samples and populations, it is essential to have a clear notion of what these three terms really mean before we are able to interpret the results of the statistical tests we will be covering in Chapter 4. To help further this understanding, consider the following examples.

3.2.2 Examples and illustrations

Predictions, or more properly 'hypotheses', are made throughout almost all areas of psychological research, ranging from health or clinical psychology to educational or occupational psychology. For example, psychologists interested in establishing new findings in the field of criminology or forensic psychology might predict that a new rehabilitation program will be more successful in preventing criminal behaviour than an existing program. Similarly, educational psychologists with an interest in new and innovative approaches in educational psychology may predict that the introduction of new learning technologies such as virtual learning environments (VLEs) will have an impact on students' abilities to assimilate knowledge.

If these psychologists were to state such hypotheses formally, as part of a research proposal perhaps, then they would attempt to make these as explicit and formal as possible such as with the following:

In the case of the forensic psychologist, the hypothesis may appear as:

- 'Significantly fewer offenders on the new program will re-offend compared to those on the existing program who will re-offend',

while the educational psychologist may sate the hypothesis thus:

- 'There will be a statistically significant difference between the exam results of students who use VLEs compared to those who do not use VLEs'.

Hypotheses are stated in this explicit way in order that we may more easily relate our research results back to our hypotheses when we are interpreting those results. Generally speaking, the greater the level of clarity we have regarding our hypotheses, the easier it will be to successfully interpret out results.

As mentioned above, experimental hypotheses are classed either as directional or non-directional – and the above offers examples of both of these. The forensic, or re-offending, example illustrates the former type of hypothesis as it is predicting a particular direction which the results will take, in this case of the intervention of the program acting to reduce the re-offending rates. The educational example on the other hand illustrates the latter form of hypothesis, as it is simply predicting that there will be a difference between the performance of participants based on their exposure to the VLE, without saying whether this is expected to be an improvement or a decline in that performance.

However, technically – and somewhat counter-intuitively – it is not the experimental hypothesis which is the focus of analysis. Rather it is the *null* hypothesis which is the focus of analysis. Indeed, the experimental hypothesis is often termed as the 'alternate' hypothesis. The null hypothesis simply states that there will be no effect – with the above examples, for instance, that there would be *no* improvement in re-offending rates, or *no* difference in exam results – and it is one of the aims of our research to use the results of our data analysis to enable us to reject (or not reject) such a null hypothesis. This is where we apply the notions of probability and statistical significance – they allow us to reject (or not reject) the null hypothesis with a certain level of certainty. Again, it can be something of a challenge for us to conceptualize this approach when we first encounter this notion of the null hypothesis, so as with before a summary table might help (Table 3.2).

We can again turn to the classic example of coin-flipping to help us explain these concepts. If we know that we have a standard coin, we know that there is an equal 50:50 chance of it landing either heads or tails. If we flipped the coin a hundred times, and it landed heads up fifty times, this would be exactly as expected. If it landed forty times heads and sixty times tails, then we still might think that this is pretty much as expected. Perhaps even a 30:70 ratio would be within the expected range of outcomes? However, if, for every hundred flips of the coin it landed heads up twenty times

Table 3.2 Examples of null, experimental, directional hypotheses

	Forensic psychology example	Educational psychology example
Null hypothesis	There will be no significant difference between the re-offending rates of those on the new as compared to the existing program	There will be no statistically significant difference between the results of those on the VLE as compared to the non-VLE module
Experimental hypothesis	Significantly fewer offenders on the new program will re-offend compared to those on the existing program	There will be a statistically significant difference between the exam results of students who use VLEs compared to those who do not use VLEs
Direction	Directional (1-tailed)	Non-directional (2-tailed)

(in other words a one in five chance) we might start to be surprised; and if it was just ten times (a one in ten chance) we might start to think it was a dodgy coin – but where would we draw the line and conclude that there was sufficient evidence to indicate that the coin *is* dodgy? Just how many times out of a hundred would it need to fall heads up before we conclude that something other than pure chance is contributing to this?

If we follow statistical convention we would draw this line – or set the 'significance level' – at five times out of a hundred (also expressed as 5% or more usually as 0.05). In other words, if we flipped a coin a hundred times and it landed heads up only four times then we would say that this is beyond what could be expected simply by chance and that we should indeed think that something else is causing this. More technically, we would say that this is beyond what could be expected if the null hypothesis were true. If however, the coin landed heads up only ten times, or eight times or even six times out of a hundred, we would not draw this conclusion. In other words, if we have a situation where the coin is landing heads up only 4% of the time, then this is said to be statistically significant, but that 5% or more would be deemed (at this 'alpha level' of 0.05) to be *not* statistically significant.

This coin-flipping example may seem of little relevance to psychology, but it is often used to illustrate the principles of probability and statistical significance which *are* relevant to psychology, or at least with respect to the process of hypothesis testing. When we conduct statistical tests we are calculating the probability of a result occurring if the null hypothesis is true, in other words the probability of a result occurring when there is no statistically significant effect. When this probability or 'p-value' is below 0.05 then the result is said to be statistically significant and we reject the null hypothesis. If the p-value is 0.05 or above, then we do not reject the null hypothesis.

As part of the discussion on probability, it should be noted that the alpha level (or 'criterion' as it is also known) is not always set at 0.05. Studies which have reported results at the 0.01, or even the 0.001 level (i.e. one chance in a thousand) are sometimes seen in the literature. Additionally, you may find some studies reporting the results of their research as being significant at the alpha level of 0.1 (i.e. one in ten), although this is increasingly rare.

Before moving on from this, it is also worth mentioning that this approach is not totally foolproof, and there is always the possibility that we may reject the null in error – that is, when we have concluded that there is a statistically significant result but where in reality this is not the case. The converse of this occurs when there is actually a significant effect taking place, but where our results have led us to conclude that there is not – in other words a situation where we do not reject the null when we actually should.

These two scenarios are known as the Type I and Type II errors (see Table 3.3), and can be more formally stated thus:

- Type I: We reject the null when it is actually true (i.e. we conclude there is an effect when there is not)
- Type II: We fail to reject the null when it is not true (we conclude that there is not an effect when there is).

The risk of these Type I and Type II errors is directly influenced by the alpha level that has been set. For example, setting the alpha

Table 3.3 Summary table of Type I and Type II errors

		H_o is actually:	
		True	False
H_o is:	Not rejected	Correct	Type II error
	Rejected	Type I error	Correct

level at 0.1 increases the chance of a Type I error, while setting at 0.001 increases the chance of a Type II error. Note that it is usual to state that either the null is rejected or not rejected – it is not usual to state that we accept the null (or that we accept or reject the experimental).

3.2.3 Further reading

Field, A. P. (2005). *Discovering Statistics Using SPSS (and Sex, Drugs and Rock 'n' Roll)* 2nd Edition. Sage. sections 1.8.2, 1.8.3.

Holt, N. and Walker, I. (2009). *Research with People: Theory, Plans and Practicals.* Palgrave Macmillan. chapter 4.

Howitt, D. and Cramer, D. (2008). *Introduction to Research Methods in Psychology* 2nd Edition. Pearson. chapter 2.

Howitt, D. and Cramer, D. (2008). *Introduction to Statistics in Psychology 4th Edition.* Pearson Prentice Hall. chapters 15 and 16.

Miles, J. and Banyard, P. (2007). *Understanding and Using Statistics in Psychology.* London: Sage. chapter 4.

3.3 Parametric assumptions

3.3.1 Concepts

The term 'parametric statistics' describes an approach to data analysis which estimates population parameters. Parametric 'assumptions' refer to the requirements which any data must meet in order that parametric statistics be used. Generally speaking there are three such requirements – that the data must have a scale level of measurement, must have a normal distribution and that in the case of independent or unrelated research designs, the groups in each condition have equal (or almost equal) variances. Each of these three assumptions is outlined below.

A scale level of measurement

This is probably the simplest factor to determine when considering the use of parametric statistics – that the data to be analysed must have been measured as a scale variable. This is an area which has already been covered in the first chapter of the book and, as mentioned in that earlier section, reflects the more sophisticated nature of the scale level of measurement. In other words that the scale level of measurement lends itself to the use of the mean as a preferred measure of central tendency whereas other levels of measurement do not.

Much of parametric statistics is based on the mean, and therefore if data are of a form where the mean cannot be used then neither can parametric statistics be used. The bottom line here is that if our dataset is composed of measures made at the nominal or ordinal level, then it is unlikely that we would be able to consider the use of parametric statistics and should instead turn to non-parametric alternatives. If our data 'are' of a scale level of measurement, however, then we can move to the next consideration, below.

A normal distribution

The normal distribution describes a distribution of scores with a central peak, which tails off equally at either side – as per the classic 'bell-shaped' curve. It is a theoretical distribution with particular mathematical properties. Most of these properties, for our purposes, we do not really need to fully understand but one thing that we do need to acknowledge is how it is defined – that is, that it is a distribution of scores which have a mean of 0 and which have a standard deviation of 1. These numerical qualities describe the perfect, symmetrical, bell-shaped normal distribution.

However, a perfect bell-shape is not actually needed for us to assume that a variable is normally distributed – some deviation (or violation) from such bell-shaped perfection is acceptable. The question is how much can a distribution of scores deviate from the perfect normal distribution before it is no longer considered as normal? To answer this we need to check its skew and kurtosis. These are concepts which are commonplace in most texts and can be defined thus:

> Skew refers to the left and right asymmetry of the distribution, and is considered as either positive (with most scores being found on the left) or negative (with most scores being found on the right). If the two halves of the bell-shape are perfectly symmetrical, the skew is zero.

> Kurtosis refers to the extent of 'peakedness' or 'pointyness' in the distribution. Very sharp peaks in the distribution are a sign of high kurtosis (or leptokurtosis) while flat distributions are signs of low kurtosis (or platykurtosis).

Remember, the skew and kurtosis of a distribution represent its departure from the classic normal distribution, that is, that the larger the value for skew or kurtosis, the less 'normal' we can consider that distribution to be. Therefore, both skew and kurtosis need to be within reasonable limits for normality to be assumed. The cut off point, where skew and kurtosis are considered *too* big, is calculated by some simple arithmetic – that is, both need to be less than twice their respective standard errors. Thus, if the skew and kurtosis are within two standard errors, a normal distribution can be assumed. As this involves a little mental arithmetic and numerical manipulation (but not too much!), a simple example of this is given in Table 3.4.

Equal variances

The third assumption to be met when considering the use of parametric tests refers specifically to the case of data collected via studies of an independent or between groups design, that is, where there is more than one group of participants or where there are different participants included within each level of the independent variable. The equal variances assumption states that the distribution of scores around the mean of the two groups of participants in a between groups study should be approximately equal. Thus, the distribution of the scores around the mean for those in Group A, should be the same as that for those of Group B.

Equality of variances is usually determined by conducting the Levene test. This test gives a value known as F, the size of which indicates the extent of the difference in the variances – the greater the value of F, the greater the difference between the variances of the two groups (with a Levene F-value of 0 indicating zero difference between the variances). Thus, the greater the value of F, the less comparable the variances of the two groups become and the less likely we are able to consider the data for analysis via parametric tests.

As with the case of the skew and kurtosis above, we do not actually need a 'perfect' score of 0 to consider that this assumption of equal variances is met. We are able to accept some deviation of this, but just as before, the question arises as to how large this value of F can become before we consider this as being too large. Luckily, this does not require any mental arithmetic on our part, and is actually calculated for us when using some of the tests of the more popular statistics programs. This calculation (which is part of the pretesting process) is often carried out alongside the main statistical test – most notably alongside the calculation for the independent t-test – and because of this it is covered in more detail in the section dealing with this test (in Section 4.1). For now it is probably sufficient just to acknowledge the importance of the Levene test, and to remember that the smaller the F-value it produces then the better this is for purposes of parametric testing.

So in summary of the above, before conducting parametric tests on our data we need to know a little about their characteristics and that they conform to certain assumptions. Firstly that they represent a scale level of measurement, secondly that they have acceptably low values of skew and kurtosis, and thirdly (in the case of between group design) that they score a low F-value on a Levene test meaning that the variances can be considered as being equal. Let's consider an example of all this...

3.3.2 Examples and illustrations

Perhaps one of the most often quoted examples of a dataset suitable for parametric statistics in psychology is that of IQ scores – and if we consider a simple illustration, such as comparing the IQ scores of students at two fictitious universities (Uni. A with Uni. B, as illustrated in Figures 3.2 and 3.3), we should be able to see why. By the way, IQ is considered here to be a scale variable, as is usually the case (see Babbie 2006; Wimmer and Dominick 1987) – though note that some other sources sometimes dispute this (e.g. Sheskin 2003). Rather than dwell on the nature of IQ, or even of how to undertake such measurements or of how to produce charts and tables such as those which follow (remember the emphasis on this guide is non-numerical!) it would probably be more productive to focus on their interpretation. It may also be a good idea to not pay too much attention to so many of the students at each of these universities having such low IQ scores!

If we examine the following charts, each of a spread of IQ scores, we can see that they look rather similar. The curve which has been superimposed over the histogram indicates that they both appear to be approximately normally distributed, and also with very similar distributions around the mean. However, we should really

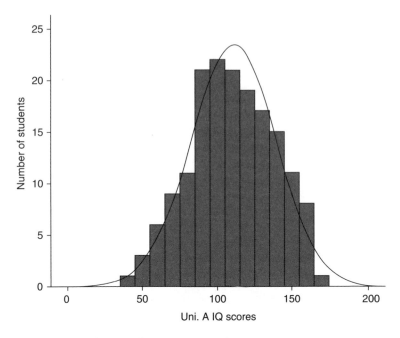

Figure 3.2 Distribution of IQ scores at Uni. A

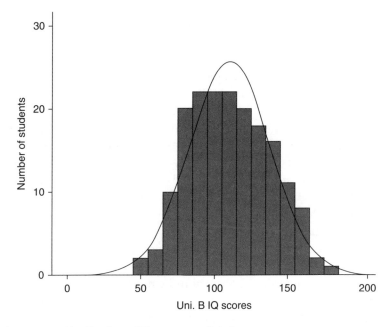

Figure 3.3 Distribution of IQ scores at Uni. B

check this via more objective means. In other words, we should check the skew and kurtosis of each dataset to establish the extent of any deviation from normality in either university's set of scores. We should also then check the Levene statistic to ensure that any difference between the universities in terms of their variances is not statistically significant.

Table 3.4 illustrates the outcome of the pre-checking in this case, via the output from the SPSS program (we will be referring to several more of these outputs throughout the next chapter). This output demonstrates that the skew and kurtosis of both sets of scores are within acceptable limits. In other words, that the skew and kurtosis for each of the two groups in our dataset is less than twice their respective standard errors.

It can also be seen, from the lower part of the table, that the Levene statistic (of 0.1) representing the difference between the variances of the two groups is too small to be of statistical significance (p = 0.75) and that they can therefore be considered equal. This output therefore confirms for us that the parametric requirements have been met.

The results of these pretests, when taken together with the scale level of measurement of the IQ data, therefore indicate that we have sufficient evidence to support our assertion that we do indeed have data here which are suitable to be analysed via parametric tests. If our aim is to determine if there is a statistically significant difference between the IQ scores of the two universities we would choose a parametric test of difference for a between groups, two-condition design (i.e. the independent t-test, covered in the next section).

Table 3.4 Results of tests for normality (via skew and kurtosis) and equal variances (via Levene)

	N	Mean	Skewness		Kurtosis	
	Statistic	Statistic	Statistic	Std. Error	Statistic	Std. Error
A_IQ_scores	166	110.54	.047	.188	−.258	.375
B_IQ_scores	177	110.79	.159	.183	−.659	.363
Valid N (listwise)	166					

	Levene Statistic	df1	df2	Sig.
IQ_Scores Based on mean	.101	1	341	.751

Although the pretesting of data for these notions of scale, normality and equal variances are essential for accurate parametric testing, they do tend to seem a bit mechanical after a while, and are therefore not always reported in research publications to a great extent. However, they are invariably carried out prior to testing and instances of their (albeit usually minor) mention in journal papers can be found without much difficulty. A few examples of this are outlined below.

The first, in keeping with the above theme of intelligence and ability, concerns a study conducted by Lyn et al. (2005a) which investigated sex differences on the WISC-R (Wechsler Intelligence Scale for Children – Revised) of over a thousand 11-year olds. The study was comprised of a series of ability measures such as Picture Completion, Coding, Similarities, Block Design, Object Assembly and Mazes. The researchers found that boys obtained significantly higher scores on some of these subtests (e.g. similarities) while girls were found to significantly outperform boys on others (e.g. coding) as per the results of the independent t-tests administered to the sample. Prior to the t-tests being used, however, the researchers undertook pretesting to establish the parametric nature of the data being collected. The Levene test for equality of variances was run and indicated that the variances were not significantly different for any of the subtests and IQs apart from the subset of Block Design, on which the variance for boys was found to be significantly greater than that for girls. Standard independent t-tests were therefore computed assuming equality of variances for all subtests *except* Block Design, for which alternative testing was used.

In a subsequent paper, the same authors ran a study similar to the above (Lyn et al. 2005b), only this time with an increased sample size of 1,400 children, who were of a much younger age (three years old). Once again a series of subsets were administered, along with measures for Verbal IQ, Performance IQ and Full Scale IQ. The researchers used t-tests to analyse the data, with the results confirming those of previous studies which found that among preschool children girls have significantly higher IQs along various measurements than do boys. Of concern here, though, is the pretesting – and once again prior to calculating the values of t, the Levene test was administered and showed that the variances of the girls and the boys were not significantly different for any of the ability measures. As no differences in variance were found, this fulfilled the homogeneity of variances criterion for parametric testing and thus allowed the researchers to continue with the main analysis of the data via t-tests.

A slightly different IQ-related study was carried out by Cassady (2004) which examined differences between male and female participants in terms of IQ test anxiety rather than the IQ test results themselves. The researcher performed pre-checks on the data prior to undertaking parametric testing via t-tests. Values for kurtosis and skewness were examined as well as the distributions of scores for each of the variables under study. These analyses demonstrated that the responses conformed to the assumption of normal distribution. Once parametric assumptions had been satisfied, the researcher employed the use of an independent t-test to establish if there were any sex differences in the recorded tests of anxiety. In this case none were found. This in itself represented a form of pretesting, used by the researcher to establish that no significant differences were to be found between men and women, so that all subsequent analyses could be conducted on the sample as a whole, without the concern that any significant differences found could have been due to sex of the participant. All subsequent analyses then used the combined responses of male and female participants.

3.3.3 Further reading

Howitt, D. and Cramer, D. (2008). *Introduction to SPSS in Psychology 4th Edition*. Pearson Prentice Hall. chapter 4.

Howitt, D. and Cramer, D. (2008). *Introduction to Statistics in Psychology 4th Edition*. Pearson Prentice Hall. chapter 4.

Miles, J. (2001). *Research Methods & Statistics*. Crucial Publishers. chapter 8.

3.3.4 Narrative

As it just wouldn't seem right to conclude a chapter without at least a passing reference to our intrepid reaction time researcher, perhaps we can take this opportunity to consider some of the considerations which he should perhaps make before embarking upon an inferential analysis of the data he has collected so far.

For example, in terms of the predictions or hypotheses being stated, the researcher would need to ensure a degree of clarity over whether the research was based on a directional or non-directional prediction as this has direct consequences for the analysis. For the sake of simplicity let us say that he has designed his research study to investigate a series of non-directional or 2-tailed hypotheses. For example, for Week 1 that he is investigating a significant difference between clubbers and non-clubbers, but he is not predicting which way this will go – that is, that either the clubbers or the TV watchers could be more alert.

In terms of the pre-checks the researcher needs to consider, firstly, the level of measurement of the data being collected. If this

Table 3.5 Aspects of the reaction time study including sampling and suitability for parametric testing

Week	Study	Design	Level of measurement	Central Tendency	Spread	Representative	Pre-checks
1	Expt.	Between	Scale/ continuous	Mean	SD	Std. Err.	Normal dist. & Eq. variances
2	Expt	Between	Ordinal/ discrete	Median	Range/ IQR	N/A	N/A
3	Expt	Between	Nominal/ discrete	Mode	N/A	N/A	N/A
4	Expt	Within	Scale/ continuous	Mean	SD	Std. Err.	Normal dist.
5	Expt	Within	Scale/ continuous	Mean	SD	Std. Err.	Normal dist.
6	Non-Expt.	Within	Scale/ continuous	Mean	SD	Std. Err.	Normal dist.

is assumed to be nominal or ordinal, as in the case of the sessions held on Weeks 2 and 3, then he need go no further down the parametric route. In the case of Weeks 4, 5 and 6, he will need to consider the distribution of the scores in order to ensure that the they meet the criterion of a normal distribution, while for Week 1 he will need to consider both the normality of the distribution and also whether the variances of the groups in the two conditions can be considered as equal. These considerations are included in the 'Pre-checks' column of Table 3.5.

Before steaming ahead with any parametric testing, then, the researcher would need to run a few checks, as illustrated by the Tables 3.6, 3.7 and 3.8. Table 3.6 indicates that the scores of the non-clubbing sample could be said to be more representative of

Table 3.6 Standard error figures for the clubbing and non-clubbing samples

		N	Mean	SD	
Activity		Statistic	Statistic	Std. Error	Statistic
Clubbing	Reaction_time	10	292.00	29.090	91.990
	Valid N (listwise)	10			
Non-clubbing	Reaction_time	10	204.00	20.177	63.805
	Valid N (listwise)	10			

Table 3.7 Skew and kurtosis figures for the clubbing and non-clubbing samples

		N	Skewness		Kurtosis	
Activity		Statistic	Statistic	Std. Error	Statistic	Std. Error
Clubbing	Reaction_time	10	.304	.687	−1.418	1.334
	Valid N (listwise)	10				
Non-clubbing	Reaction_time	10	.543	.687	−.512	1.334
	Valid N (listwise)	10				

Figure 3.8 Use of the Levene statistic to check for comparable variances

		Levene statistic	df_1	df_2	Sig.
Reaction_time	Based on mean	3.243	1	18	.089

the population than the scores of the clubbing sample. Table 3.7 shows that the distributions of the scores collected during week one for both groups are within acceptable limits of skew and kurtosis and can therefore be considered as approximating to a normal distribution. While, for the final pre-check here, the value of the Levene statistic in Table 3.8 indicates that there is no significant difference between the variances of the clubbing and non-clubbing groups (p=0.09), and that these variances can therefore be considered as equal.

Indications are therefore that the data fulfil the requirements for parametric testing, and that the researcher can now launch himself into a series of parametric analyses, as detailed in Section 4.1 (as well as a number of non-parametric analyses in Sections 4.2 and 4.3).

3.5 Summary

In Chapter 3 we began with an acknowledgement that psychologists are rarely in a position to conduct research on entire populations as this would often entail negotiating access to very high numbers of potential participants, which would in turn entail a great deal in terms of cost, time and effort. As an alternative, we as researchers can utilize statistical procedures and sampling techniques to enable us to infer the characteristics of a given *population* from the characteristics of a representative *sample* (hence the term *infer*ential statistics), and we are able to gauge just how representative such a sample really is via its *standard error* (i.e. the smaller the standard error, the more a sample is representative of the population).

This chapter has also considered the notion of *hypothesis testing*: of forming predictions, either directional or non-directional, of potential relationships between variables or of how different treatments of an Independent variable may have an effect on measurements of a Dependent variable. The chance or likelihood that such an effect will be observed was discussed in terms of *probability* (i.e. the probability that a predicted effect will take place), before introducing the concept of *statistical significance* – which really refers to the likelihood of the observed effect occurring for reasons other than pure chance.

These concepts of hypotheses, probability and statistical significance were discussed in some detail as part of this 'bridging' chapter, as along with an understanding of samples and populations, it is necessary to have a clear notion of their meaning and inter-relationship before progressing to the chapter on inferential statistics. Also of critical importance to understanding the procedures outlined in that final chapter – and thus also covered here in Chapter 3 – is the distinction between parametric and non-parametric testing.

Generally speaking inferential statistics can be divided into two varieties, the more powerful *parametric* tests and the less powerful *non-parametric* equivalents. The choice of the latter over the former is usually made due to the data to be analysed failing to meet three specific requirements – that the it must have a *scale* level of measurement, that it must be *normally distributed* and that (in the case of unrelated research designs) the data in each condition have *equal variances*.

This understanding of parametric assumptions really represents the last piece of the puzzle in terms of preparations for inferential stats. Once we have (1) a clear notion of the characteristics of the data in terms of its ability to meet these three requirements, (2) are able to construct hypotheses and interpret the results of statistical tests in order to reject (or not) reject the null, and (3) are able to gauge how likely such sample-based findings will represent effects in the wider population, then we will be able to (4) proceed to the final chapter of the book and to feel confident in being able to tackle all the tests and procedures contained therein!

1. Which of the following terms best describes the sentence: 'In a blind-tasting, people will not be able to tell the difference between margarine and butter'.

   a. A directional hypothesis.
   b. An operational definition.
   c. A null hypothesis.
   d. An experimental hypothesis.

2. The assumption of homogeneity of variance is met when:

   a. The variance in one group is twice as big as that of a different group.
   b. Variances in different groups are approximately equal.
   c. The variance across groups is proportional to the means of those groups.
   d. The variance is the same as the interquartile range.

3. What is a significance level?

   a. The level at which statistics finally become interesting.
   b. The impact that reporting statistics incorrectly could have.
   c. A pre-set level of probability that the results are correct.
   d. A pre-set level of probability at which it will be accepted that results are due to chance or not.

4. A Type I error occurs when:

   a. We conclude that there is a statistically significant effect when there actually is not.
   b. We conclude that there is not a statistically significant effect when there actually is.
   c. We conclude that our inputs and data entry are wrong.
   d. We conclude that our outputs and test results are wrong.

5. Another term for non-parametric tests is:

   a. Non-normal tests.
   b. Data-free tests.
   c. Non-continuous tests.
   d. Distribution-free tests.

6. Levene's test tests for whether:

   a. Data are normally distributed.
   b. The variances in different groups are equal.
   c. The assumption of sphericity has been met.
   d. Group means differ.

7. What is the conventional level of probability that is often accepted when conducting statistical tests?

   a. 0.1.
   b. 0.05.
   c. 0.5.
   d. 0.001.

8. A null hypothesis:

   a. States that the experimental treatment will have an effect.
   b. Is rarely used in experiments.
   c. Predicts that the experimental treatment will have no effect.
   d. None of the above.

9. 'Sleep deprivation will reduce the ability to perform a complex cognitive task'. State the direction of this hypothesis:

   a. Directional.
   b. Non-Directional.
   c. Both.
   d. Not enough information given.

This chapter covers the particular area of statistics which is probably the one most associated with difficulties for first year psychology students, that is, *inferential* statistics, where we go beyond simply summarizing data and move toward establishing the relationships between variables and generalizing from samples to populations. However, this need not be an area necessarily associated with said difficulties. If you have understood what the book has said so far with no major problems, and have been able to follow the format – concepts, everyday examples, excerpts from the literature and so on – up until this point, then this final chapter should present no particular difficulties. Also, as explained in the preceding chapter, most of the difficulties with statistics which are experienced by psychology students tend to centre on the lack of preparation for the inferential aspects (hence the inclusion of the previous 'prelude' chapter) rather than difficulties with the inferential procedures themselves.

This final chapter may even look a little shorter than expected, particularly given the importance of inferential statistics to most first year psychology courses. This is partly due to the format taken – as with the book so far, this chapter aims to cut out the lengthy numerical explanations given by most texts in order to focus on the verbal descriptions and to emphasize the conceptual understanding of the area. However, it may also be due because, once we have established the nature of our data via the processes we have discussed in the chapters up until this point, then the choice and execution of the specific test in accordance with the nature of that data is relatively mechanistic. It should, in theory, be a matter of the pieces of the puzzle simply falling into place (or in other words, once we have gained all the information necessary to navigate the decision-making process, the rest is just a matter of tracing the connections to the appropriate end point). In other words, the successful implementation of inferential statistics is mostly in the preparation!

This chapter is comprised of the now familiar aspects of concepts, examples and illustrations. These have been applied throughout the structure in accordance with three perspectives or considerations which need to be observed in selecting correct parametric tests.

The first perspective concerns the three main levels of measurement we use to measure data in psychological research, nominal, ordinal and scale, as first detailed back in Chapter 1. This consideration of the level of measurement is reflected via the three main layers of the chapter, that is, scale in 4.1, ordinal in 4.2 and finishing off with nominal in 4.3. Within each of these layers can be found the second perspective, that of research design. Thus the chapter's structure reflects not only the three data types we encounter in psychological research, but also the design considerations which we make, that is, whether we are adopting a within-groups or a between-groups design framework – as covered back in 1.2. This is because an understanding of both level of measurement and research design is essential to following the correct inferential procedures. The chapter's final perspective reflects the fundamental nature of research questions themselves– of whether we are conducting research which aims to uncover differences or similarities, that is, it orients the selection of inferential testing either to tests of difference or tests of correlation.

These three elements thus lead to the chapter structure below – which should hopefully now be seen to be fairly logical – a consideration of the analytical procedures suitable for investigating differences between groups, differences within groups, and the correlation of variables. Section 4.1 deals with the parametric variants of each of these, while Sections 4.2 and 4.3 deal with the ordinal and nominal (i.e, both non-parametric) variants respectively.

One thing to note here is the conventional treatment given to correlation as regards how tests of correlation are usually defined. There is some difference of opinion here among various texts on research methods, and it is sometimes challenging to know where to best place correlation in a guide to statistics, especially where one is aiming to be concise rather than comprehensive. Some texts

Table 4.1   Organization and structure of Chapter 4

	Difference between	Difference within	Correlation
4.1. Scale	Independent t-test	Paired t-test	Pearson
4.2. Ordinal	Mann-Whitney	Wilcoxon	Spearman
4.3. Nominal	Chi square	McNemar	N/A

restrict the topic to the descriptive statistics sections, some to the inferential sections (Breakwell et al. 2006), some as a measure of association alongside chi square (McQueen and Knussen 2006) and still others in a dedicated chapter all of its own (Field 2005). This guide has opted to place correlation alongside the difference testing, as this enables easier comparisons to be made between them. One other point to note, by the way, concerns the gap in the above table relating to tests of correlation for nominal data. These do actually exist (e.g. Cramer's phi coefficient), but their use by undergraduate psychologists is so rare that such analyses have not been included here.

4.1 Parametric testing

Section 4.1. offers an outline description of each of the two-condition parametric tests most frequently encountered on the first year of a psychology undergraduate course. It also notes the assumptions which must be met in order to use these tests – that is, tests which are designed for data collected on a scale level of measurement – firstly in terms of tests of difference (for both between and within designs) and then in terms of tests of correlation.

4.1.1 Concepts

Difference: between groups (the independent t-test)

When our dataset conforms to the parametric assumptions that we have detailed in the previous section, and we are interested in comparing two sets of data to establish any significant differences in their respective means, then the test we should choose is the independent t-test (also known as the unrelated, unpaired, between groups, or uncorrelated t-test).

It differs from its sister test, the paired t-test, in that it tests for statistically significant differences between means of two conditions when the participants in one condition are *not* the same as the participants in the other. The use of the Independent t-test is thus applicable in situations where:

- The data are held in two conditions
- The participants in the first condition *are not* also in the second condition
- The data in both conditions are of a scale level of measurement

- The data in both conditions are normally distributed
- There is no significant difference between the variances of the data in each condition

Difference: within groups (the paired t-test)

The paired t-test, as with the independent t-test, is used with data which satisfy all parametric assumptions, and, again just as with the previous test, is used to establish whether the overall difference between the means of the two sets of scores is large enough to be considered statistically significant. It differs from the former version in that it is used only in cases where the participants in the first condition are also the participants in the second condition. The use of the paired t-test is thus applicable in situations where:

- The data are held in two conditions
- The participants in the first condition *are* also in the second condition
- The data in both conditions are of a scale level of measurement
- The distribution of the differences between the two conditions is a normal distribution

Correlation (the Pearson product-moment correlation coefficient)

This differs from the above tests and approaches in two fundamental ways. Firstly, its focus is upon similarity, or co-relationships, as opposed to a focus on difference. Secondly, it is not based on the notion of dependent and independent variables.

The tests so far have been based on measuring the value of a dependent variable at two levels of an independent variable (i.e. the two conditions), and testing for any significant differences between the means of the dependent variable at these two levels. Correlation, however, is based on measuring the extent of relationship between two *separate* variables. The previous distinction of dependent or independent variable is thus not made. However, it should be noted that regression analysis, based on the same principles as correlation, does differentiate the two variables by referring to them as *predictor* and *criterion*.

One final feature of correlation which should be clarified is that it *cannot* be used to infer causation – even if it is shown that there is a significant relationship between two variables this does not mean that one causes the other. The most common method of testing the size and degree of correlation between two variables is the Pearson product-moment correlation coefficient, or more commonly known simply as the Pearson correlation coefficient. Its use is thus applicable in situations where:

• The data are held in two conditions, each a separate variable
• The participants in the first condition are also in the second condition
• The data in both conditions are of a scale level of measurement
• The data in both conditions are normally distributed

4.1.2   Everyday examples

Difference: between groups (the independent t-test)

A common practice within many university departments, especially those with large cohorts, is to divide the coursework assignments received from students into batches to be marked by different members of staff. This allows the whole submission-marking-returning of assignments process to be (theoretically!) completed more quickly and efficiently, although it does present an extra task for the module leaders in that they need to ensure that all the markers are marking to the same standard or to the same marking criteria.

One of the ways in which to ensure that this required level of consistency is being maintained is to conduct an appropriate test of difference on the batches of marks which have been awarded by each of the markers. In other words, to determine if there is any statistically significant difference between the means of each set of marks. In practice, this process usually involves the analysis of several batches of marks, as around four or five markers per assignment is not uncommon – and indeed it can sometimes be many more – but for our purposes we'll just assume that there are two. Any more would require a different test – Analysis of variance – which is not actually covered here!

So, we already know that this data would be of a scale level of measurement, but the other characteristics of these two sets of marks would need to be checked via the aforementioned methods, that is, using the Levene test to check equality of variances, and the 'two standard errors' rule to check for a normal distribution. (Actually, the distribution of marks in student assignments is often found to be approximately normal – most marks being distributed around the centre with the number decreasing either side of this, to the point where very few students attain very high marks and very few attain very low marks.) Once the equal variances and normal distribution requirements had been confirmed, then the choice of most appropriate test would be the t-test.

The independent t-test: typical SPSS outputs

The tables below show a number of outputs typically produced by SPSS when dealing with an analysis such as that above. The first table (Table 4.2) illustrates the mean values of the dependent variable for the two conditions of the independent variable (in this case giving the average exam marks awarded by each of the two markers) and also shows the skew and kurtosis results for each. In this instance, the marks appear to be rather similar, with the first marker giving just a few marks more on average than the second. In order to see if this difference should be considered as being statistically significant, we would use the independent t-test but only after conducting the pre-checks required to ensure that it can be used.

Table 4.2   Means, skew and kurtosis of the two samples

		N	Mean	Skewness		Kurtosis	
Marker		Statistic	Statistic	Statistic	SD	Statistic	SD
Marker 1	Marks	10	59.40	−.138	.687	−1.387	1.334
	Valid N (listwise)	10					
Marker 2	Marks	10	54.80	.084	.687	−1.034	1.334
	Valid N (listwise)	10					

The first of these, the pre-check for a normal distribution, can be easily performed via a little mental arithmetic, that is, by applying the 2 × SE rule (see Section 3.3.1). The tables below show that the skew and kurtosis figures for the marks given by both markers are well within their respective 2 × SE parameters, and so we can accept the distribution of both sets of scores as being normal.

Next we should test for equality of variances by checking on the Levene figure. SPSS does this in a rather odd way. Even though the Levene test is something of a 'pre-check' to be carried out before proceeding with a t-test, SPSS encourages us to carry out the Levene and the actual independent t-test simultaneously, resulting in the Levene result being output at the same time and in the same table, as that of the t-test. This can be a little confusing at first, but just remember that the 'F' and the first 'Sig.' refer to the results of the Levene test, while the remainder of the table then refers to the results of the independent t-test. The 'F' and the first 'Sig.' values of Table 4.3 do indeed indicate that there is no statistically significant difference between the variances (F = 0.465, p = 0.504). The variances can therefore be considered as equal, thus fulfilling this requirement for the use of the t-test.

Having established that the requirements of a parametric test have all been fulfilled – that is, the equal variances, normal

Table 4.3   Results of the Levene and the independent t-test

		Levene's test for equality of variances		T-test for equality of means						
									95% Confidence interval of the difference	
		F	Sig.	t	df	Sig. (2-tailed)	Mean difference	SD	Lower	Upper
Marks	Equal variances assumed	.465	.504	1.413	18	.175	4.600	3.256	−2.240	11.440
	Equal variances not assumed			1.413	17.515	.175	4.600	3.256	−2.254	11.454

distribution and the scale level of measurement of the exam marks – we can simply read off the results from the first line of the above table. This tells us that the difference between marks awarded by the each of the markers is not actually statistically significant (t = 1.41, df = 18, p = 0.175) - and that therefore the module leader is saved on this occasion from having to perform any major moderation procedures.

(The results of the analysis could thus be expressed as t = 1.41, df = 18, p = 0.18 [2-tailed]).

Difference: within groups (the paired t-test)

Results of 'before and after' type studies are frequently reported in the media, in articles and TV shows and documentaries, although these are admittedly of varying levels of scientific credibility! Although all too often there is a lack of the nitty-gritty details, most of the results of such studies are probably derived – or at least should be derived – via the paired t-test. Semi-serious TV programs which aim to improve people's health or fitness, for example, would fall into this category. Typical dependent variables could be based on measurements such as comfortable walking distance (in km) before and after a fitness program, or weight (in kg) before and after a diet program. Any program aiming to demonstrate the benefits of such training or dieting should really reveal whether any improvements found in the 'after' condition over that found in the 'before' stage represent an actual statistically significant change. The same essential idea applies to a few other TV shows dotted here and there, such as the monetary values applied to the 'before and after refurbishment' conditions on property shows – although admittedly these are much less likely than the health-based shows to offer supporting evidence for improvement in the form of statistical results.

The feature which all such shows or articles have in common is that they are examining changes measured on a scale level of measurement, and tend to focus on the same individuals in both the before and after conditions. One also assumes that as so much is made of how the encouraging results of the studies can be applied to those reading the articles or watching the TV shows that thorough checks upon the normality of the distribution are also being carried out. If this were to be the case, then all conditions would be met to make full use of the paired t-tests, in order to more effectively support the claims of improved health or increased financial values which were being made.

The paired t-test: typical SPSS outputs

Below we have a trio of SPSS tables typical of the outputs of a paired t-test. The initial table (Table 4.4) shows the results of the central tendency and dispersion calculations, giving us the mean and standard deviations for each of the 'before diet' and 'after diet' conditions. We can see that there is some difference here, in that the mean weight following the diet appears to be less than that before the dieting took place. Indeed, the average weight of the participants appears to have dropped by 2.5 kg.

To determine whether this weight loss is statistically significant, we would need to conduct a paired t-test, but not before we run the usual pre-checks. In this case, we are already aware that we have a scale level of measurement (the dependent variable of participants' weight as measured in kilograms), and that we do not need to check for equal variances (as this is a within-groups design). However, we do still need to consider the distribution of the scores – or more accurately the distribution of their differences, as illustrated in Table 4.5.

Table 4.4 Means and SDs of the two conditions

		Mean	N	SD	SE mean
Pair 1	Before_diet	122.70	10	5.293	1.674
	After_diet	120.20	10	6.303	1.993

Table 4.5 Skew and kurtosis of the differences

	N	Skewness		Kurtosis	
	Statistic	Statistic	SE	Statistic	SE
Differences	10	.612	.687	.492	1.334
Valid N (listwise)	10				

Table 4.6 Results of the paired t-test

		Paired differences							
					95% Confidence interval of the difference				Sig. (2-tailed)
		Mean	SD	SE	Lower	Upper	t	df	
Pair 1	Before_diet - After_diet	2.500	4.327	1.368	-.595	5.595	1.827	9	.101

Table 4.5 indicates that the extent of skew and kurtosis in the distribution of the differences variable is not too large. Using the same 2 × SE procedure that we adopted in the case of the independent t-test, we can see that the distortion from a normal distribution for each of these aspects is well within two standard errors, and that therefore we can indeed assume a normal distribution. So, as all parametric requirements appear to be fulfilled, the results can now be simply read from Table 4.6.

The results of the paired t-tests in Table 4.6 indicate that there is not actually a significant difference between the two aforementioned means, and that the average weight of participants did not significantly decrease during the period in which they were following the diet. In this sense then, the average weight loss of 2.5 kg is not considered to be a statistically significant difference and does not therefore lend support to the efficacy of the diet program.

(The results of the analysis could thus be expressed as t = 1.3, df – 9, p = 0.10 [2-tailed]).

Correlation (the Pearson product-moment correlation coefficient)

Classic, everyday examples of correlation can frequently be seen all around us, and include the pairing of measures of weight and height, the time spent in lectures being paired with exam results, the number of hours of sleep being paired with next-day alertness, or even the amount of rainfall we all enjoy on an almost daily basis in the UK being paired with incidences of umbrella carrying. All these are examples of positive correlations, where an increase in the magnitude of one variable such as weight is observed to accompany the increase in another, for example, height. Negative correlations are also frequently seen or quoted and are not too difficult to conceptualize – for example, an increase in rainfall being paired with a decrease in the sales of sun cream, a decrease in the number of items of clothing worn during the summer being paired with an increase in the average daily temperature, or an increase in the price of fuel we pay being paired with a decrease in the number of miles we actually drive.

If one looks or listens closely enough, one can soon become familiar with the use of correlation in the media. Financial news reports frequently mention the impacts of the correlation of currencies or the effects of positive or negative correlations between the price of crude oil, sterling, stocks and share etc. Mention is also often heard on news reports of health-related correlations, for example, an established link between poverty and obesity (BBC News 02/11/09) and even in the world of education, where TV usage is often found to be negatively correlated with academic performance (Morrison 2009). Each of these involves a scale level of measurement (weight, income, currency, time) and, assuming that the dispersion of such measurements resembled that of a normal distribution, would be considered suited to the Pearson correlation coefficient.

The Pearson correlation coefficient: typical SPSS outputs

The typical SPSS outputs for our third and final parametric test appear in Table 4.7. For this illustration, we have taken as an example the television and test score relationship mentioned above, this relationship being the focus of a correlational study aimed at determining whether or not television watching is actually associated with lower exam scores.

Table 4.7 Skew and kurtosis results of the two variables

	N	Skewness		Kurtosis	
	Statistic	Statistic	SE	Statistic	SE
TV_hours	20	−.448	.512	−.801	.992
Test_scores	20	−.114	.512	−1.187	.992
Valid N (listwise)	20				

As with the previous tests, the first table represents the results of the pretests which are usually made in order to ensure that our data meets parametric requirements. Table 4.7 thus indicates the extent to which the dispersion of the two sets of scores departs from a normal distribution. Using the now familiar 2 × SE rule, we can see that the scores on both our variables – TV hours and test scores – do indeed conform to a normal distribution, with the skew and kurtosis of each being within the acceptable 2 × SE limits. Thus, as the normal distribution requirement is met, and as both the variables are being measured on a scale level of measurement, we can proceed with examining their relationship via the Pearson correlation coefficient.

The second of the two tables here represents the results of the actual correlation itself. Table 4.8 thus gives us the value of the coefficient, r = .149, as well as the p value which in this case is 0.53. This allows us to draw the conclusion that there actually seems to be a positive relationship between TV viewing and test scores, that is, that those scoring higher on the test are also those who watch the most television. This is indicated by the r value of .149 being a positive rather than a negative value. However (and this is the big however!), the p value tells us that although TV hours and test scores appear to be positively related, this is not statistically significant. Indeed, the p value here of 0.53 is many times larger than the standard alpha 'cut-off' level of 0.05. This lack of a significant relationship is illustrated by the final figure in our Pearson outputs, the scatter plot (Figure 4.1), which clearly

Table 4.8 Results of the Pearson correlation coefficient

		TV_hours	Test_scores
TV_hours	Pearson Correlation	1	.149
	Sig. (2-tailed)		.530
	N	20	20
Test_scores	Pearson Correlation	.149	1
	Sig. (2-tailed)	.530	
	N	20	20

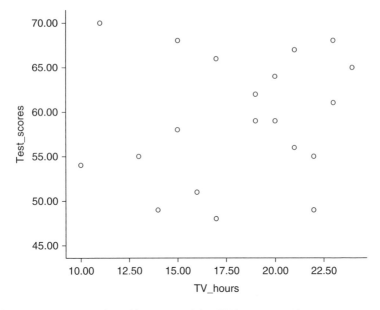

Figure 4.1 Scatter plot of hours watching TV by test results

demonstrates the lack of any strong relationship between these two variables.

(The results of the analysis could thus be expressed as r = .15, N = 20, p = 0.53 [2-tailed]).

4.1.3 From the literature

Difference: between groups (the independent t-test)

There follows three illustrations from the psychological literature which should help to demonstrate the situations where the use of the independent t-test is deemed appropriate. All three studies are based on observational procedures, although with rather different perspectives – of observing aggressive behaviour, observing pro-social behaviour, and of observing the use of interpersonal space or positioning. All were considered suitable for unrelated t-test analyses due to the nature of the research question, the design and the level of the data being collected.

1. Bandura, Ross and Ross (1961)

Aims and methods

A study with which you are probably already well familiar made use of the independent t-test in order to investigate differences between male and female participants. In this case, the participants were groups of boys and girls aged between three and six years old, and the differences being investigated were related to the instances of aggressive behaviour being displayed by each group. In other words, the research was aimed at investigating how the level of aggression in boys differs from that of girls. If you have guessed that this was an aspect of the previously mentioned Bandura et al. (1961) study, then you would be right. In addition to simply observing and recording instances of aggressive behaviour in children following exposure to specific visual stimuli, Bandura also split the sample so that he was able to probe further, to establish whether boys in the sample were more aggressive than girls, or vice versa.

Choice of test

Bandura and his associates were able to use the t-test as an analytical technique to uncover sex differences for these particular types of aggressive responses due to the parametric nature of the data which had been collected. In other words, the data conformed to a scale level of measurement (i.e. it was comprised of equal distances between each point on the scale), was of a normal distribution and with both groups displaying equal variances.

Results

Bandura and his associates were interested in various aspects of aggression, including both physical and verbal, that were displayed by the children. The initial results indicated that boys reproduced more imitated physical aggression than did girls ($t = 2.50$, $p < 0.01$), but that there was no significant difference as regards their imitated verbal aggression. The researchers probed further still, also investigating the interactive effect between the sex of the participant and the sex of the model. In other words, whether boys reacted more aggressively than girls after viewing an aggressive *male* model, and whether the girls reacted more aggressively than boys after viewing an aggressive *female* model. The researchers indeed found a significant interaction effect in the case of male model and male participant, with boys exhibiting more physical (t = 2.07, p < 0.05) and verbal (t = 2.51, p < 0.05) imitated aggression following exposure to an aggressive male model than did the girls. The girls exposed to the aggressive female model performed more aggressively than did the boys, but not to the same degree (i.e. this was not found to be a statistically significant effect).

The researchers examined the data from additional perspectives to those outlined above, with the aim of determining if there were any further interactive effects, such as an overall test of the influence of the sex of the model in the film clip that is, one which incorporated all measures. However, this was prevented due to limitations in the data, particularly the skewed distributions of scores of participants, leading to the data being considered unsuitable for parametric testing in these areas. Bandura et al. therefore turned to non-parametric approaches to analyse the data in these cases, using techniques which will be described in the Section 4.2.

2. Sprafkin, Liebert and Poulos (1975)

Aims and methods

While Bandura's experiments have become infamous as studies of learned aggressive behaviour, a slightly later investigation demonstrated a similar effect only this time being based on learned *pro-social* behaviour. A study by Sprafkin et al. (1975) certainly bore certain similarities to the early work of Bandura, inasmuch as visual clips were played to child participants who were then observed so that the researchers could note their resultant behaviour. The Sprafkin et al. study, however, differed in that it employed the use of actual television programmes as the independent variable, with instances of subsequent helping behaviour being recorded as the dependent variable. By using actual TV programmes, the researchers would therefore be able to demonstrate a clearer or more direct link between observed and actual behaviour, and thus also the effect which television may have on those who were viewing.

The participants in the study were exposed to one of three television programmes. Firstly, an episode of Lassie which clearly demonstrated the benefits of altruism (in this case of a boy helping a dog), secondly a further episode of the same series but one which was devoid of such helping behaviour and finally, an episode of an entirely different series known as the Brady Bunch (which was considered by US audiences at the time to represent a comedy).

Following exposure to the TV episode, each child was asked to sit at a console and was invited to play a rewards-based 'points game', where they could win a number of clearly visible prizes if they were able to press the correct buttons in order to light a display. The more times the correct buttons were pressed, the more points were accrued, and the closer each child came to earning the desired prize. In addition, each child was told of a nearby kennel which housed several puppies, and that the he or she would need to monitor the well-being of these puppies via a set of headphones. Quite simply, if the children were to hear the puppies barking on the headphones then they should take this as a sign of distress and should press a designated help button instead of continuing with the game. Additionally, they were to continue pressing the help button until the puppies stopped barking.

The help button was in reality a timing device, and thus represented the method of recording the dependent variable – to determine the length of time the child would try to seek help for the puppies rather than to continue with the game for their own reward. In other words the dependent variable was recorded as the number of seconds they were willing to divert their attention from activities designed for their own benefit (the prize) toward that for the benefit of others (in this case the fictitious puppies).

Choice of test

The level of measurement in this study was therefore scale, with the design being unrelated (each group of children being independent of one another). As the distribution and variances requirements for parametric testing were also satisfied, the researchers chose to use the independent t-test as the method of analysis (or at least for a number of their analyses).

Results

The results indicated that participants who watched the pro-social Lassie episode did indeed press the help button for a significantly longer duration than did those in either of the control group conditions. In the case of the pro-social versus neutral Lassie shows, the difference in the duration of the help button presses (and thus the extent of the helping behaviour) was found to be significant at the 0.05 level ($t = 2.08$, $p < 0.05$) while for the pro-social Lassie versus the Brady Bunch episode, the difference was even more marked ($t = 2.79$, $p < 0.01$), thus offering strong supporting evidence that exposure to a televised example of helping can indeed increase a child's willingness to engage in that helping behaviour.

3. Dean, Willis and Hewitt (1975)

Aims and methods

Many of the studies mentioned thus far, and their approaches to analysing their collected data, have been conducted in laboratories or controlled environments. However, such approaches are of course equally valid for the analysis of data collected via field studies. One such study was that conducted by Dean et al. (1975) which took place in a number of locations at a US Naval station. Such a location was deemed suitable to be used for testing the study's main hypothesis, that is, that personal space – or interaction distance – is influenced by perceived personal status.

Based on studies of both humans and animals which had found a relationship between the preferred distancing of two individuals based on their perceived dominant or subordinate status, the researchers chose this location as it was relatively easy to identify the dominant/subordinate relations between participants simply by virtue of their clothing (each participant thus being easily identified in terms of their rank: Captain, Commander, Lieutenant and so on), the predictions here being that there would indeed be a difference in the physical distance or 'personal space' created by the participants based on their military rank.

Choice of test

The research was conducted unobtrusively, with the military participants being unaware that they were being monitored. The actual data being recorded was the distance between individuals during conversations or other interactions. This was measured by the observers simply noting the number of floor tiles positioned between the participants in each case. As all the settings which were chosen were tiled with uniformly sized squares floor tiles, it was relatively easy to calculate the actual distance between participants for each of the observed interactions. Also, as the tiles were of a uniform number of centimetres – that is, a scale level of measurement – they could be used as the basis for parametric tests to be used with the data as the normal distribution and equal variance assumptions were met. The design of the study was obviously that of between-groups as the groups were based on military rank – and thus a participant in one group could not appear in another (simply as participants cannot hold more than one rank at any given time).

Results

The researchers did indeed find a relationship between military status and interaction distance, and that there was a general tendency for the distance between military personnel to be greater when a person of lower rank approached a personal of higher rank (t (289) = 3.18, p < 0.01) than when peers approached each other, or a person of high rank approached a person of lower rank. In other words, those of a lower rank appeared to be more cautious in their approach, and to keep their distance. The results therefore supported the notion that interaction initiated by subordinates toward dominates is characterized by a greater interaction distance than when interaction is initiated toward peers or subordinates – and also that the distance is greater when the difference between rank is greater.

Difference: within groups (the paired t-test)

Following on from the above illustrations of the independent t-test, our treatment of its sister test, the paired t-test, also makes use of three examples from the literature although with each being drawn from rather different areas. The first example illustrates how the paired t-test can be used to analyse the impact of music on anxiety, with the second demonstrating its use as part of a study on the importance of a 'good sense of humour' in our personal relationships. The final example then uses the paired t-test to consider the effects which mobile phones can have on concentration levels by utilizing the old favourite of reaction time as a dependent variable.

1. Lai, Chen, Chen, Chang, Peng and Chang (2008)

Aims and methods

The phenomenon of anxiety being experienced during the run-up to an examination is not unfamiliar to many students, and for many this can be a highly disruptive and unpleasant experience. In extreme cases, feelings of apprehension and fear may hinder optimal learning and adversely influence the student's level of performance. Research undertaken with the aim of uncovering ways to lower one's pre-exam anxiety can therefore be of some considerable interest to the student community.

One such investigation (Lai et al. 2008) has examined the impact and efficacy of music as an anxiety-reduction technique, in other words, of whether background music can have a reducing effect on the anxiety experienced by those anticipating their forthcoming exams. The study made use of both psychological and physiological changes, recording both subjective and objective measurements. It also made use of a mixed design (i.e. incorporating elements of both between-group and within-group designs) although it is the within-groups aspects that we will consider here.

The researchers examined the effects of music on examination anxiety among university students with the specific aim of comparing effects of 'music' and 'silence' conditions on those who were undergoing a modular exam. This comparison was via measurements of two dependent variables, firstly their state of anxiety and examination anxiety levels and, secondly, in terms of their pulse rates and skin temperatures.

The within-groups aspect of the research was partly based on a before and after design, with students completing subjective questionnaires on anxiety before and after taking a forty minute examination. Of most relevance to our use of this study (as an illustration of the use of the paired t-test) were the objective physiological measures of pulse rate and skin temperature which were also taken before and after the examination. Thus, the investigators were measuring two scale level variables – skin temperature as measured in degrees Celsius, and pulse rates as measured in beats per minute – as physiological indicators of arousal or anxiety levels both before and after the exam.

The before and after measures were applied to two groups of students – the first, experimental group where students were exposed to back ground music, the second, control group, where students had only silence. The analysis for this part of the experiment was therefore based on two before and after comparisons, one for each of the two groups.

Choice of test

Each of these comparisons was undertaken by using the t-test, as the design was of a within-groups or related nature. The students in the pretest condition for the silent treatment were also in the post-test condition. Similarly for the music treatment, the students being tested in the pre-exam condition were the same as those in the post-exam condition. Two sets of t-tests were therefore produced, those testing for before and after differences in (1) temperature and (2) pulse of the 'silence' students, and those testing for those same effects in the 'music' students.

Results

The results indicated that there were no significant before and after differences found for either pulse or temperature change in the silence group. However, the researchers did find that significant differences were to be found for temperature ($p < 0.001$) and pulse rate measurements ($p = 0.02$) in the music group.

2. Bressler, Martin and Balshine (2006)

Aims and methods

Anyone who has ever scanned the classifieds will have come across the acronym GSOH quite a few times. Despite a number of research findings indicating that this phrase appears with equal frequency in ads posted by both men and women, there is evidence to suggest that there is actually a sex difference in the interpretation of this phrase. Bressler and Balshine (2004) found that although both men and women expressed a preference for a partner with a good sense of humour, the extent of this differed markedly, with women seeming to genuinely appreciate a sense of humour in a partner much more than men, in other words, that men tend not to find humourous women to be particularly attractive.

To further investigate this phenomenon, Bressler, Martin and Balshine (2006) used a questionnaire-based approach to assess the importance which participants placed on their partner's 'production of humour'. They also measured the level of importance which participants placed on their partner's receptivity to their own (i.e. the participant's) humour.

Choice of test

Each participant therefore produced scores on two variables – importance of partner humour and importance of receptivity to their own humour – this therefore representing a within-groups design as each participant gave ratings to both conditions, and it was the comparison of these conditions upon which the analysis was based. The analysis was designed to look for differences between these two conditions, and so a test of difference was chosen. As the nature of the data conformed to the usual parametric requirements (the researchers actually used a transformation procedure to achieve this, but we need not worry about that now), the test chosen as being the most appropriate was the paired t-test.

Results

Results of the paired t-test indicated that the female participants valued a partner's production of humour as much as they valued a partner's receptivity to their own (i.e. the female participant's) humour [paired t-test, $t(73) = 1.10$, $p = .10$]. However, the paired t-test results for the male participants in the sample indicated a different picture; that men rated their partner's production of humour to be less important than their partner's receptivity to their own (i.e. male participant's) humour [$t(54) = 5.07$, $p < .001$].

As the male participants emphasized the importance of their partners' receptivity to their own humour higher than did the female participants, one could conclude that men have a different take on the value of the GSOH than do women – that when they stress the importance of humour in their potential relationships they may be referring not so much to the sense of humour of their (female) partner, but more to their partner's appreciation of the (male) participant's *own* sense of humour.

3. Patten, Kircher, Östlund and Nilsson (2004)

Aims and methods

Investigations into reaction time are often used as illustrations of the paired t-test, due to the transparently scale nature of the data being recorded (i.e. the dependent variable invariably being measured on the scale level of milliseconds). One such investigation involving reaction times being recorded within a related (within-groups) design was the study conducted by Patten et al. (2004), aimed at establishing the ways in which mobile phone use can impact upon driver concentration and distraction.

The acknowledgement that the use of mobile phones while driving leads to significant levels of driver distraction has been reflected in recent years by legislation limiting or banning their use while driving a vehicle. Less attention however has been paid to just how this level of distraction occurs – with regard to the actual conversation taking place (and its level of complexity) and other events taking place simultaneously (e.g. tuning a radio or interacting with others within the vehicle). Similarly, less attention has been paid to the details of the ways in which the driver physically interacts with the mobile phone, that is, the extent to which using a hand-held phone differs from a hands-free phone with regard to the relative impact these can have upon driver concentration.

Choice of test

In order to investigate these factors, this study employed a simulated driving situation, where forty participants completed a theoretical motorway route while being required to engage in one of two standardized phone conversations via one of two standardized phone interfaces. The researchers thus investigated the effect of two independent variables here – type of conversation (either simple or complex) and type of phone (either hand-held or hands-free). The participants who took part in the simple conversation condition also took part in the complex condition, similarly, those taking part in the hand-held condition also took part in the hands-free condition, thus making this a within-groups design.

The impact of manipulating these levels of independent variable was assessed by measuring the time that participants took to react to a light stimulus (LED) which appeared within his or her visual periphery. The reaction time measured was the time taken for the participant to press a small switch attached to the left index finger, the data being recorded in milliseconds. As the data were of a scale level of measurement, and as the distribution of difference scores was found to approximate to a normal distribution, the paired t-test was chosen as the most appropriate test of differences.

Results

The results indicated that there was a significant effect of conversation type but no effect of telephone mode. The results of the paired t-test found significant differences in reaction time between the simple and complex conversation levels for both the hand-held ($t = -8.036$; $df = 39$; $p \leq 0.001$) and hands-free ($t = -7.414$; $df = 39$; $p \leq 0.001$) conditions. In other words, the participants' reaction times increased when shifting to a more cognitively demanding mode of conversation, but that no benefit of hands-free over hand-held mode of interaction was found.

These findings therefore suggest that the content of a mobile phone conversation is a more important factor affecting driving and driver distraction than that of the type of telephone being used. The more difficult and complex the conversation, the greater the possible negative effect on driver distraction.

Correlation (the Pearson product-moment correlation coefficient)

Moving away from parametric tests of difference, we now consider tests of association or correlation for data which are considered to conform to parametric assumptions. Two illustrations of the Pearson correlation coefficient are therefore provided below. The first considers measurements of a physiological nature, where the Pearson has been used to establish the relationship between physiological structures and spatial knowledge or abilities. The second derives from the field of psychometrics, where the Pearson has been used in order to assist in the validation of a developing research instrument – this being a frequent use of the correlation coefficient in psychological research.

1. Maguire, Gadian, Johnsrode, Good, Ashburner, Frackowiack and Frith (2000)

Aims and methods

A study of the physiology of the brain offers us an interesting example of both a correlational study and also of the use of the Pearson correlation coefficient. With a view to uncovering more detail concerning the role of the posterior and anterior hippocampi in memory formation, Maguire et al. (2000) sought to uncover any relationship between the characteristics of this brain structure and the possession of a certain form of knowledge – that is, of whether individuals possessing certain knowledge also posses hippocampi of increased size or density relative to that of individuals who do not possess such knowledge. The knowledge which was used as the basis of this study was in fact *the* knowledge – the information held within the minds of London taxi drivers following the extensive training period whereby they are required to memorize all London street names, notable locations and routes.

In order to qualify as an approved driver of one of the classic London black cabs, each taxi driver must first acquire an internal representation of the complex London road system; a cognitive map of spatial relationships which allows taxi drivers to navigate from one point to another not only by the most direct route, but to alternate such routes in the event of traffic jams and other disruptions. This knowledge therefore represents a relatively standardized representation of spatial relationships and memories held by these particular participants which are not held by the population in general. By conducting MRI (Magnetic resonance Imagery) scans of both taxi drivers and non-taxi drivers, the researchers were able to detect any differences in brain structure between the two groups – and a statistically significant difference was indeed observed: a greater volume of grey matter was found in the posterior hippocampi of taxi drivers than in that of control participants, while a lesser volume of grey matter was found in the anterior hippocampi of taxi drivers than those of the non-taxi driving control group.

However, the researchers were not only interested in the physiological differences between the brains of taxi drivers and non-taxi drivers (which would require the use of a test of difference, such as the independent t-test above); they were also interested in determining any effects within the taxi drivers themselves. In the investigation outlined here, the researchers were primarily looking for any relationship between physiology of brain structures and the length of time which taxi drivers had actually held 'the knowledge'. They therefore aimed to test for whether more experienced taxi drivers were in possession of larger of more dense structures (in this case hippocampi). In other words, they tested the hypothesis that as the length of time a person spent as a taxi driver increased, so too did the size and density of their hippocampi – that is, that increased hippocampi density occurs alongside increased taxi-driving experience.

This is clearly very different to the tests previously mentioned, which invariably sought to test for differences between groups – differences presumably initiated by the manipulation of an independent variable. In the correlational element of the Maguire et al. (2000) study, there is no such manipulation – nobody is manipulating the length of service of taxi drivers, and certainly nobody is manipulating the size of the hippocampi by engaging in brain surgery. Indeed with a correlational design, we usually state that there is no independent variable, but that we are merely measuring two dependent variables (in this case experience and hippocampi size) in order to determine their relationship.

Choice of test

The researchers chose the Pearson correlation coefficient to test their hypothesis that the two dependent variables were interrelated, as both variables conformed to the required parametric assumptions. The level of measurement of taxi-driving experience was considered as being scale as this variable was based on the number of weeks, months and years spent in the job (it was thus a measure of time or duration – which is always considered as scale). The level of measurement of the hippocampi was based on MRI reading of volume – another measure considered to be scale.

Results

The results of this element of the study did indicate significant relationships between the extent of driving experience, or 'length of knowledge', and brain structure, although only with regard to the right hippocampus; the researchers identified a significant positive relationship between right posterior hippocampus volume and driving experience (r = 0.6, p < 0.05) while there was a significant negative relationship between that of right anterior hippocampus size and driving experience (r = –0.6, p < 0.05).

Despite this finding, that there is an association between taxi-driving experience and hippocampus size, it is difficult to draw any further inferences. It is not possible for example to conclude that taxi-driving leads to an enlargement of the right posterior hippocampus. We could just as easily conclude that people with this hippocampus configuration have a tendency to become taxi drivers, and that those with the largest right posterior hippocampus tend to stick with the job for the longest. Either or neither of these inferences could be the case, but due to the very nature of correlation (i.e. that it does not imply causation) we cannot be certain which.

2. Windle (2004)

Aims and methods

Correlation coefficients are often found in psychology not just in their own right (i.e. as a means of analysis of data to support one's predictions as in the case above) but also as a means by which further measures or research instruments may be developed and validated. For example, it is commonplace to test the reliability of a newly developed test by applying the test to the same participants at various points in time and then determining the degree to which the findings over time correlate with one another. A high degree of correlation over time supports the view that the newly developed test is reliable.

A research paper by Windle (2004) reports on just such a use of the correlation coefficient. The author cites several sources supporting the view that high levels of alcohol use among students is becoming a concern with respect to the health effects which this may have, and propose that in order to better understand the patterns and nature of this use among the student population, more needs to be known about students behaviour prior to enrolment. In other words, they proposed to investigate this relatively unexplored 'pre-student' area which may be of potential value in the early identification of increased risk.

As it is not practicable (or perhaps not possible) to directly access this information – that is, to research the students on these issues for a period of perhaps several years *prior* to their enrolment – some form of retrospective measure would need to be employed, that is, one where current students give an account of their past behaviour or activities prior to becoming a student.

This study thus employed a research instrument aimed at determining retrospective use of alcohol, incorporating questions which were designed to assess key elements of alcohol use, including the frequency and quantity of use, binge drinking and drinking style (e.g. steady, social or weekend). However, before considering the results produced by such an instrument, the researchers sought to establish its reliability by determining whether or not there was a significant test–retest correlation. In other words, of whether students who responded with a particular answer during the first data collection stage then responded with the same (or a very similar) answer during the second data collection stage.

Choice of test

The reliability of the survey items for the instrument, or their stability over time, was evaluated by the use of the Pearson correlation coefficient. The Pearson was chosen as an appropriate measure as the responses to the questions were clearly of a scale level of measurement – for example, the number of days in a month during which alcohol was consumed, the number of drinks consumed on these days, and the number of days in a month during which more than five drinks were consumed are all examples of a measurement scale based on equidistant points.

Results

The values of the Pearson correlation coefficient (r) for each pair of items ranged from .71 to .96, the correlation between each item pair being found to be statistically significant in each case ($p < 0.001$). These findings therefore provided strong support for the reliability of this retrospective research instrument, and according to the researcher indicated a level of reliability that was equivalent to similar retrospective assessments of alcohol use which have been developed for other (i.e. non-student) populations.

4.1.4 Narrative

Now that we've looked at a few real-life examples of psychological studies which have incorporated the three parametric tests which we are covering in this chapter, we could perhaps revisit our own ongoing hypothetical illustration of statistical procedures by considering once again the reaction time scenarios first introduced way back in the first chapter of the book. With various tweaks made to the design and to the measurements being taken in these scenarios, we should be able to see how each of the aforementioned tests (and those we have yet to encounter) could be applied to the data analysis.

Difference: between groups (the independent t-test)

If we think back to this hypothetical investigation first described in Section 1.1.4, remember that we have initially a situation where there are two conditions, each being comprised of a different group of participants – clubbers and non-clubbers. Each group is being assessed on their performance of a reaction time task with the resultant outputs being measured in milliseconds; in other words a scale level of measurement. The first thoughts here are probably to use an independent t-test to determine if there is a statistically significant difference between the two groups, but we really should check on the two other parametric requirements first.

Let's say there were ten participants in each condition, who each produced reaction time results as listed in Appendix 1 (the non-numerical nature of this book has successfully kept them out of the main text!). The results of the normal distribution checks are shown in Table 4.9. A quick examination of the skew and kurtosis figures within the table indicates that for both conditions a normal distribution can be assumed, as the skew and kurtosis values for both the clubbing and non-clubbing groups are less than twice those of their respective standard errors.

This table also includes the mean reaction times for the two groups – we can see that the clubbers on average were slower than their non-clubbing counterparts. This initial table thus gives us the direction of any difference being found, although of course we do not yet know if this difference is of any statistical significance.

The next table (Table 4.10) gives the result of both the Levene's tests for equal variances and the independent t-test itself. As mentioned previously, SPSS outputs the pretest Levene result at the same time as that of the main independent t-test, resulting in two significance values. To help reduce any confusion with these, the sig. value for the pretest is at least positioned to the left of the sig. value for the main test. From Table 4.10, we can see that the 'F' and the first sig. value do indeed indicate that there is no statistically significant difference between the variances (F = 3.24, p = 0.09). The variances can therefore be considered as equal, thus meeting this requirement for using the independent t-test.

The final criterion for the t-test, that of a scale level of measurement, is already assured as we know that milliseconds represent scale level data. We would at this point, therefore, finally be ready to read off the result of the t-test and to find that we do actually have a significant difference here between the two groups. In other words, that there is a statistically significant difference between clubbers and non-clubbers in terms of their reaction times, with this difference indicating that clubbers are way slower!

(The results of the analysis could thus be expressed as t = 2.49, df =18, p = 0.02 [2-tailed]).

Table 4.9 Means, skew and kurtosis of the two samples

Activity		N	Mean	Skewness		Kurtosis	
		Statistic	Statistic	Statistic	SE	Statistic	SE
Clubbing	Reaction_time	10	292.00	.304	.687	−1.418	1.334
	Valid N (listwise)	10					
Non-Clubbing	Reaction_time	10	204.00	.543	.687	−.512	1.334
	Valid N (listwise)	10					

Table 4.10   Results of the Levene and the Independent t-test

		Levene's test for equality of variances		T-test for equality of means						
									95% Confidence interval of the difference	
		F	Sig.	t	df	Sig. (2-tailed)	Mean difference	SE	Lower	Upper
Reaction_ time	Equal variances assumed	3.243	.089	2.486	18	.023	88.000	35.402	13.622	162.378
	Equal variances not assumed			2.486	16.032	.024	88.000	35.402	12.962	163.038

Difference: within groups (the paired t-test)

Just as with the above example, we could again revisit the familiar earlier reaction time scenarios, this time paying our attention
to Weeks 4 and 5 events of the study as described in Section 1.2.4.
This differs from the above only in that the design is now of a
within-groups nature. This would therefore imply, as the data are
still of a scale level of measurement, that the paired t-test would
be required.

The 'pre-checks' here are a little different, and perhaps a little
simpler as there is no need to check for equal variances between
groups (as the two conditions this time comprise the same individuals). However, there is a slight difference in the process of checking for a normal distribution, as this time we need to check not on
the distribution of the two sets of data as such, but on the distribution of their differences. In other words, we need to first subtract
the Week 4 data from the Week 5 data to create a new variable
of 'differences' and then run the normality checks (via skew and
kurtosis) on this differences data.

For those wishing to pursue the logic of this, the rationale
underpinning this procedure is explained in more detail in
Howitt and Cramer (2008c, chapter 12). Here, however, we will
just focus on the interpretation of the outputs. Table 4.11 indicates that the extent of skew and kurtosis in the distribution of
the differences variable is not too large, that is, the distortion

from normality for each of these aspects is less than two standard errors.

As we can now conclude from the skew and kurtosis figures
that we do indeed have a normal distribution of differences, and
as we already know that the data is of a scale level of measurement, we are in a position to go ahead with the t-test, as illustrated in Table 4.12. This output, with its t value of 2.62 and a
p value of 0.03, indicates that there is (perhaps unsurprisingly)
a statistically significant difference between the means of the
groups at Week 4 and Week 5. The table's mean value of 88 tells
us that this difference is based on the Week 5 (non-clubbing)
results being an average of 88 seconds faster than the (clubbing) results from the previous week, thus supporting the view
that Thursday nights out have the effect of slowing down Friday
mornings reaction time.

(The results of the analysis could thus be expressed as t = 2.62,
df = 9, p = 0.03 [2-tailed]).

Table 4.11 Skew and kurtosis of the differences

	N	**Skewness**		**Kurtosis**	
	Statistic	Statistic	SE	Statistic	SE
Differences	10	.115	.687	.536	1.334
Valid N (listwise)	10				

Table 4.12 Results of the paired t-test

		Paired differences							
					95% Confidence interval of the difference				
		Mean	SD	SE	Lower	Upper	t	df	Sig. (2-tailed)
Pair 1	Clubbing (Wk 4)-Non-clubbing (Wk 5)	88.000	106.333	33.625	11.934	164.066	2.617	9	.028

Correlation (the Pearson product-moment correlation coefficient)

To conclude this section, we could again consider scenario 2.1.3, this time looking at the activities of Week 6, where the researcher decided upon taking a different approach to the analysis, and instead of investigating potentially significant differences in the results he decided to look at potentially significant similarities. He thus considered the groups' reaction time results alongside that of the number of hours spent out on the town the previous night.

This form of analysis would therefore require a very different approach due to (1) the nature of the aim, or research question – that is, looking for similarities not differences – but also due to (2) the nature of the variables. In this case the focus would not be on two levels of an independent variable as with the above tests, but rather it would be looking at two separate variables – reaction times and the period of time in previous night 'party-mode'.

As both these variables are comprised of a scale level of measurement (i.e. milliseconds and hours are both measurements which conform to an equidistant scale) then we would, normal distribution permitting, make use of the Pearson correlation coefficient here. As usual, the normal distribution could be checked via the two standard errors rule, as in Table 4.13, which indicates that the skew and kurtosis of the two variables are such that both variables are indeed within the limits of what could still be considered as a normal distribution.

As we have now ensured that the parametric requirements have been fulfilled, we can look at the general relationship between the two variables via a scatter plot and further, to examine whether this relationship is of statistical significance, via the Pearson correlation coefficient (denoted as 'r').

Table 4.13 Skew and kurtosis results of the two variables

	N	Skewness		Kurtosis	
	Statistic	Statistic	Std. Error	Statistic	Std. Error
Party Time (Hrs)	10	.485	.687	−.693	1.334
Reaction time (ms)	10	.304	.687	−1.418	1.334
Valid N (listwise)	10				

The scatter plot of Figure 4.2 certainly suggests a positive relationship between the two variables, that is, that as the number of hours spent out on a Thursday night increases, so too do the number of milliseconds required to react to a computer task on a Friday morning. The implication here being that the longer spent out on the town of an evening, the slower one reacts to stimuli the following morning.

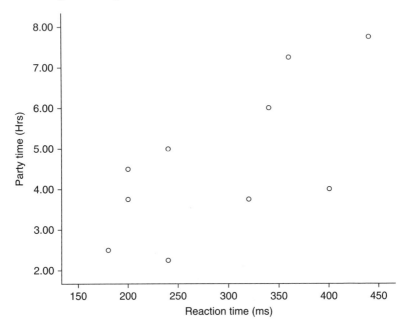

Figure 4.2 Scatter plot of the relationship between reaction time and 'party time'

Table 4.14 Results of the Pearson correlation coefficient

		Party time (hrs)	Reaction time (ms)
Party time (Hrs)	Pearson correlation	1	.685*
	Sig. (2-tailed)		.029
	N	10	10
Reaction time (ms)	Pearson correlation	.685*	1
	Sig. (2-tailed)	.029	
	N	10	10

* Correlation is significant at the 0.05 level (2-tailed).

The scatter plot does not however tell us whether this relationship is of any statistical significance. For this we need to examine the results of the Pearson coefficient in Table 4.14, which indicates that this is indeed a statistically significant difference – the SPSS output in this case not only giving all the relevant figures but clearly stating their statistical significance with the use of a well placed asterisk.

(The results of the analysis could thus be expressed as $r = .69$, $df = 10$, $p = 0.03$ [2-tailed]).

The above section may appear to have been a little on the large side relative to what follows, due in no small part to its incorporation of material on the pre-checks which need to be performed prior to the actual testing when using parametric techniques – but hopefully this will at least have clarified the steps in these processes. Sections 4.2 and 4.3 in contrast will be rather shorter, due to the very nature of non-parametric testing with ordinal and nominal data – that is, that pre-checks are not required!

4.1.5 Further reading

Brace, N., Kemp, R. and Snelgar, R. (2009). *SPSS for Psychologists 4th Edition*. Palgrave Macmillan. chapter 3, sections 1, 2 and 3 and chapter 4, sections 1, 2 and 3.

Field, A. P. (2005). *Discovering Statistics Using SPSS (and Sex, Drugs and Rock 'n' Roll)* 2nd Edition. Sage. sections 7.5, 7.6.

Holt, N. and Walker, I. (2009). *Research with People: Theory, Plans and Practicals*. Palgrave Macmillan. chapter 4.

Howitt, D. and Cramer, D. (2008). *Introduction to SPSS in Psychology 4th Edition*. Pearson Prentice Hall. chapters 7, 10 and 11.

Howitt, D. and Cramer, D. (2008). *Introduction to Statistics in Psychology 4th Edition*. Pearson Prentice Hall. chapters 6, 7, 12 and 13.

4.2 Non-parametric testing (ordinal)

Section 4.2 is structured to mirror the approach taken in the previous section but with reference to the tests used where parametric assumptions fail to be met. It thus describes the non-parametric equivalents to the aforementioned t-tests and Pearson correlation coefficient, namely the Wilcoxon signed ranks, the Mann-Whitney and the Spearman rank order correlation coefficient. As before, each of these is covered in terms of the assumptions which must be met in order that they be used, everyday illustrations of situations in which they may be applicable, and representative examples of their use in the psychological literature.

4.2.1 Concepts

Difference: between groups (the Mann-Whitney U-test)

The most frequently used non-parametric equivalent of the independent samples t-test is the Mann-Whitney U. This is usually employed when we have a dataset comprising of ordinal data, or alternatively scale data that does not meet the requirements of equal variances or normal distribution. It should perhaps be noted that another non-parametric equivalent which is sometimes used in these conditions is the Wilcoxon rank sum test – but this should not to be confused with the Wilcoxon signed rank test, outlined below. The use of the Mann-Whitney is thus applicable in situations where:

- The data are held in two conditions
- The participants in the first condition *are not* also in the second condition

- The data in both conditions are of an ordinal level of measurement OR
- The data in both conditions are of a scale level of measurement but violate the assumptions of normality and equal variances

Difference: within groups (the Wilcoxon signed ranks test)

The Wilcoxon signed rank test is among the most frequently used non-parametric alternatives to the paired t-test. It focuses upon the size of the differences between paired observations and also their signs, for example, whether the first observation in a pair is greater or less than the second. It simply takes the paired observations, calculates their differences, ranks them from the smallest to the largest by absolute value and then adds the ranks associated with positive differences, giving the final statistic. It is thus applicable where:

- The data are held in two conditions
- The participants in the first condition are also in the second condition
- The data in both conditions are of an ordinal level of measurement OR
- The data in both conditions are of a scale level of measurement but violate the assumption of a normal distribution

Correlation (the Spearman rank order correlation coefficient)

The non-parametric version of the Pearson correlation cocfficient is the Spearman rank order coefficient (or Spearman's rho). This tends to be much less frequently used than the Pearson coefficient. It should be remembered that just as with the Pearson correlation, the Spearman can only establish whether a relationship exists, it cannot establish the *cause* of this relationship. The use of the Spearman correlation coefficient is applicable in situations where:

- The data are held in two conditions, each a separate variable
- The participants in the first condition are also in the second condition

- The data in both conditions are of an ordinal level of measurement OR
- The data in both conditions are of a scale level of measurement but are not normally distributed

4.2.2 Everyday examples

Difference: between groups (the Mann-Whitney U-test)

Data of an ordinal level of measurement is often collected by psychologists who are interested in people's opinions, attitudes or beliefs, using a scale with a limited number of points, usually no more than five or seven. For example, if we were interested in establishing the extent to which readers of this book found it useful for navigating their statistics module, we could use a scale of 1-to–5, with one representing 'not at all useful', and five representing 'very useful' and so on. If we were interested in a comparative investigation of this topic, we could ask readers to rate this guide on the aforementioned scale, and also to rate the (differently authored) guide from the previous year, also using this aforementioned 1-to-5 scale. Determining if there were any statistically significant differences between the ratings for the two guides could then be achieved via the Mann-Whitney test.

Psychologists are not alone in their use of attitude scales, however, and readers may be more familiar on a day-to-day basis with the market researchers who may be located within shopping malls, pedestrianized town centres or even knocking on householder's doors. The research topics may range from intended voting behaviour at the next election to preferences for particular types of jam, with the responses being subdivided into various divisions based on sex, age or occupational status. Regardless of the content or topics under study, however, if the research question is aimed at establishing differences (e.g. between men or women or between young or old respondents) and attitudinal data are collected along scales such as the 5 point measurements of those above, then the final analysis will be very likely conducted via the use of the Mann-Whitney U-test.

Table 4.15 Mann-Whitney ranks

	Book	N	Mean rank	Sum of ranks
Ratings	This book	10	11.40	114.00
	Last year's book	10	9.60	96.00
	Total	20		

Table 4.16 Mann-Whitney statistics[a]

	Ratings
Mann-Whitney U	41.000
Wilcoxon W	96.000
Z	−.741
Asymp. Sig. (2-tailed)	.459
Exact Sig. [2*(1-tailed Sig.)]	.529[b]

[a] Grouping variable: book.
[b] Not corrected for ties.

The Mann-Whitney U-test: typical SPSS outputs

If we use the aforementioned 'this book versus last year's book' example as an illustration of the Mann-Whitney test, we could obtain a SPSS output such as that below. As can be seen from the 'ranks' table (Table 4.15), the book is indeed scoring somewhat higher in terms of its popularity with students than the book which was being used during the previous year.

However, as encouraging as this may sound, this does not appear to be a statistically significant difference. The test statistics within Table 4.16 indicate a 2-tailed p value of 0.46 here, which is a long way from the conventional alpha of 0.05, so we can perhaps conclude from this that the book, as popular as it is, still has considerable room for improvement.

(The results of the analysis could thus be expressed as U = 41.00, $N_1 = 10$, $N_2 = 10$, p = 0.46 [2-tailed]).

Difference: within groups (the Wilcoxon signed ranks test)

An earlier example (in 4.1.2) mentioned the widespread increase in the number of 'improvement' shows on TV these days, including those which encourage us to improve the internal or external appearance of our houses, cars or even the appearance (or confidence or self-image) of their owners. The basic premise of these shows is of a 'before' condition (of a near-derelict house or an individual with low self-esteem), an intervention of some form then being made, to be followed by an 'after' condition (of a much improved shiny home or a drop-dead gorgeous inhabitant). Putting the ethics of all this aside for a moment, to ascertain whether these measures of painting and decorating our houses (or ourselves) were having any effect, we would need to make use of a test for a within-groups design as we would have the same house/person/dodgy-old motor in both the before and after conditions. The test would also need to be for an ordinal level of measurement – because the ratings used would essentially be attitudes or opinions of how much better the living room now looks, or how much more confident someone feels by getting back into that old pair of jeans – and as there is no guarantee that a subjective rating change from, say, one to two is the same 'distance' as a subjective rating change from two to three, we would need to assume an ordinal level of measurement. An appropriate test to be used in these circumstances would therefore be the Wilcoxon signed ranks test.

The Wilcoxon signed rank test: typical SPSS outputs

For the ordinal within-groups example, we could consider the case of one of the 'improvement' initiatives mentioned – a makeover show for example. As one of the incentives of such shows is to improve or enhance the feelings of self-confidence which are experienced by those receiving the makeover (and which presumably take place because of the intervention of said makeover), the success could be gauged by asking those receiving this makeover to complete questionnaires indicating their perceived levels of self-confidence both before and after this intervention. A sample dataset for this is included in the Appendix, with the outputs from the analysis of this data (via the Wilcoxon signed ranks test) shown below.

The ranks table (Table 4.17) summarizes the differences in the before and after ratings. It shows that for three of the

Table 4.17 Wilcoxon ranks

		N	Mean rank	Sum of ranks
Confidence_after	Negative ranks	0[a]	.00	.00
Confidence_before	Positive ranks	7[b]	4.00	28.00
	Ties	3[c]		
	Total	10		

[a] Confidence_after < Confidence_before.
[b] Confidence_after > Confidence_before.
[c] Confidence_after = Confidence_before.

Table 4.18 Wilcoxon test statistics[a]

	Confidence_ after - Confidence_before
Z	−2.646[b]
Asymp. Sig. (2-tailed)	.008

[a] Wilcoxon signed ranks test.
[b] Based on negative ranks.

participants there was no change in the self-confidence rating (i.e. the figure for 'ties'). It also shows that for the remaining seven participants, all rated themselves as more confident after the intervention (seven positive ranks, and zero negative ranks). The effect of this is indicated in the test statistics table (i.e. Table 4.18), which shows that the confidence-enhancing effect of the makeover was indeed statistically significant, with a p value of 0.008.

(The results of the analysis could thus be expressed as $Z = -2.65$, $N = 10$, $p = 0.008$ [2-tailed]).

Correlation (the Spearman rank order correlation coefficient)

For the final ordinal level test to be considered here, we could return to the world of education (and also to another opportunity for plugging this book!). We have already visited these areas in terms of a test of difference above, for example, looking for significant differences in the 'usefulness' of this book as compared to another, previously set text. If we changed this aspect of 'difference' to 'similarity', then we should have some material for an illustration of the Spearman correlation coefficient.

For example, we may be interested in how the views on the efficacy of this book, as measured via the same ordinal 1-to-5 scale as in the example above, relate to the performance on a statistics module of those using the book. The performance measurements in this case could be comprised of ranks or positions of users in the end of year statistics exam – those positioned first, second, third and so on. These two variables – of ratings and rankings – would thus conform to an ordinal level of measurement, leading us to select the Spearman correlation coefficient for the analysis rather than the Pearson.

More everyday examples of correlation based on ordinal data could include the product ratings to which we have now all become so accustomed on Amazon and various other websites. Such ratings have been shown to correlate positively with higher sales (Stuart 2009). Similarly in the world of online auction sales, a seller's feedback ratings as reported by online e-buyers may have a marked correlation with the final auction selling price (Lucking-Reiley et al. 2007). In each of these cases, we have scale level data in the form of prices or sales figures, but ordinal level measurement with the actual ratings.

The Spearman rank order correlation coefficient: typical SPSS outputs

For the final set of SPSS outputs in this section, we can consider some hypothetical data concerning the 'useful' ratings of this guide, and aim to determine if this has any relationship with the end of year exam performance, as mentioned above. For both these variables, the numerical coding has assumed that 'lower' equates to 'better', so the most 'useful' rating (i.e. very useful) is one, similarly the highest ranking (i.e. being first in the class) is also rated as a one.

The scatter plot (Figure 4.3) in this example presents a reasonably clear picture of the relationship between the two variables, suggesting that it is both positive and strong. When we examine the correlations table in Table 4.19, we can see that there is indeed a strong relationship and that this is actually statistically significant at the $p < 0.01$ level. In other words, there is a significant positive relationship between the two variables, indicating that the

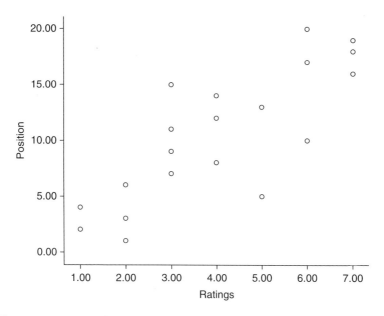

Figure 4.3 Scatter plot of the relationship between test ranking and book ratings

Table 4.19 Results of the Spearman correlation coefficient

				Position	Ratings
Spearman's rho	Position	Correlation coefficient		1.000	.813**
		Sig. (2-tailed)			.000
		N		20	20
	Ratings	Correlation coefficient		.813**	1.000
		Sig. (2-tailed)		.000	
		N		20	20

** Correlation is significant at the 0.01 level (2-tailed).

rating given to the book does indeed associate with positioning in the stats exam.

(The results of the analysis could thus be expressed as rho = .813, N = 20, $p < 0.001$ [2-tailed]).

4.2.3 From the literature

Difference: within groups (the Wilcoxon signed ranks test)

This section presents three illustrations of the use of the Wilcoxon test taking from the literature on the interaction of psychology and educational technology. The first considers attitudes toward learning generally via computers as opposed to paper-based media, the second takes a more narrow focus by concentrating on a particular technological implementation of learning, that is, podcasting, while the third considers the increasingly popular phenomenon of virtual learning environments, or VLEs.

1. Noyes and Garland (2005)

Aims and methods

It is no secret that in recent years we have seen an unprecedented growth in the adoption of information and communication technologies, in areas as diverse as grocery shopping to social networking to distribution of music and other media. Education is another area where there has been considerable change, although perhaps of an evolutionary rather than revolutionary nature. It is certainly the case that students in higher education make much more use of online reading materials in the form of electronic journals, uploaded lecture notes, digitized materials and so on, than in previous years. It may even be the case that electronic sources may soon overtake traditional paper-based sources. With such a radical shift away from the traditional approach to 'reading for a degree', it is not surprising that many psychologists are interested in the ways in which these changes are impacting on the student experience. Indeed, many are conducting research into not just the objective aspects of these changes (e.g. visual perception, ability to assimilate information via screen as opposed to paper) but also on the subjective experiences of students engaged in reading from, and in some cases listening to, a variety of digital hardware.

One such study focusing on the subjective appraisal is that of Noyes and Garland (2005). The researchers in this case were primarily focused on eliciting the attitudes of students (N = 217) toward reading and studying via computers as opposed to books. They employed a questionnaire as the research instrument, comprised of ten separate bipolar scales oriented toward rating attitudes to books and computers. Included within these ten scales were dimensions such as likeable/unlikeable, calmness/tension and comfort/discomfort. Statements relating to each of these dimensions were rated along a 7-point Likert-style scale, these points lubelled as 'extremely, moderately, slightly, neither, slightly, moderately, extremely', with each participant indicating the extent to which he or she agreed with each statement as relating to books and computers.

Choice of test

All the student participants therefore rated in both conditions (for books and computers) making this a within-groups design. As there could be no assurance of equidistance between each of these points (e.g. that the difference between extremely and moderately would be just the same as that between moderately and slightly) the level of measurement was assumed to be ordinal, and thus a non-parametric test was chosen. As with the previous example, the test chosen was the Wilcoxon signed ranks – considered the most suitable non-parametric test of difference for a within-groups two-condition design.

Results

Upon completion of the analysis, the Wilcoxon test results supported the notion that learning via books remains preferable to learning from computer. Indeed, the participants in the study received books more favourably than computers on all ten of the scales incorporated within the research instrument, with differences being significant at the $p < 0.001$ level, most notably on the scales of likeable/unlikeable ($Z = 8.29$, $p < 0.001$) and calm/tense ($Z = -9.87$, $p < 0.001$). The overall findings thus strongly suggest that despite increasing computer usage, it seems that individuals still retain a more positive attitude towards learning via books as compared to learning via computers.

2. Lazzari (2009)

Aims and methods

While the above study was focused on eliciting student attitudes toward studying with books and computers in general, a recent study by Lazzari (2009) has investigated a more specific implementation as regards the computer aspects. Rather than to compare attitudes and views on books and computers generally, Lazzari sought to examine the impact of more explicit technologies, by eliciting student impressions of podcasting, and comparing how these relate to views on traditional note-taking. This study on the impact of new and innovative learning and teaching approaches on university courses offers us a further example of the use of the Wilcoxon signed ranks test within the domain of higher education.

Lazzari's experiment was based on the introduction of a podcasting service to an undergraduate degree syllabus, the efficacy of which was evaluated by both objective (performance) and subjective (evaluative) measures. However, it is the latter which is of interest here, as the subjective measures were assessed via a Likert-type ordinal scale.

Many of us are probably aware of the use of podcasts for entertainment purposes rather than for work or for education, and indeed their uptake – so far at least – within higher education has been relatively slow. Hence the research being undertaken both on the ways podcasting can influence performance, and on the views of the podcasting services by the end users (the students themselves). In common with other studies, Lazzari (2009) incorporated both these aspects, of performance and preference, into this investigation.

However, it is the research on student attitudes which is of most interest here – attitudes which were elicited via a standardized questionnaire focusing on the aspects of speed and efficacy of use (that studying and revising using podcasts is quicker or more effective than using textbooks or class notes) and revision potential (for both theoretical and the practical parts of the course). All data relating to the above were collected on a 5-point Likert scale, with students responding to a series of statements with values ranging from 1 (strongly disagree) to 5 (strongly agree).

Choice of test

The Wilcoxon test was considered a suitable test of difference in this case due to the design – that is, that it would be testing for differences within the same group of participants (students' views on podcasting and the same students' views on note-taking). It was also seen as being an appropriate test due to the level of measurement of the data, that is, the ordinal, 'no guarantee of equidistance' nature of the 5-point Likert-type measurements.

Results

The outcomes of the analysis painted a rather mixed picture, with preferences for podcasting in some areas but not in others. For example, although the results suggested a slight preference for the efficacy of textbooks over podcasts when studying a topic, they indicated podcasts were more significantly preferred as part of a long-term strategy for reviewing material already learned in preparation for an exam ($Z = -2.725$, $p < .05$).

The preferences seem to switch once again, however, when considering their use as last minute revision tools, with the results suggesting that there is a significant preference for notes rather than podcasts as a quick tool for revising ($Z = -2.640$, $p < .05$). This apparent discrepancy is seen by the researcher as an indication of two separate learning strategies, a long-term strategy where podcasting appears to be looked upon favourably by students, and a shorter (perhaps even a 'night before the exam') strategy, where traditional means are preferred, perhaps due to the time factor involved, that is, that scanning complete audio and video files may be perceived as a relatively time-consuming activity.

3. Vuorela and Nummenmaa (2004)

Aims and methods

As the above studies have indicated, the use of technology for instruction and assessment purposes is playing an increasingly important role in higher education. One area in which this is becoming more prevalent is that of the Virtual Learning Environment, or VLE. The term VLE is usually used to refer to a system designed to support learning and teaching within an educational environment, and which tends to be used alongside lectures and seminars in order to supplement these more traditional face-to-face classroom activities. Accessed via internal or external networks, such systems incorporate various tools such as those for communication, assessment (especially those which can be automated), administration, tracking mechanisms and even wikis, blogs and social networking functions.

As technology progresses, so does the capability of the VLE, and so too does the level of complexity in interacting with them. As such, VLEs are becoming an increasingly popular focus of research by both educationalists and psychologists in order to better understand the ways in which they are used and the factors by which students consider their interaction with them to be successful and worthwhile.

One such study, which included a variety of perspectives in its scope, was conducted by Vuorela and Nummenmaa (2004). As well as a number of theoretical perspectives it also incorporated a number of different analytical tests, and is thus mentioned not only here but in the following sections on Mann-Whitney. The particular predictions of the experiment, along with the subsequent research design, data collection and analysis which will be considered here, though, involve the Wilcoxon signed ranks test.

One of the basic aims of the Vuorela and Nummenmaa (2004) study was to directly assess the impact of introducing a VLE-based teaching element, or course, to an existing teaching programme. They did this by examining four main areas which have been previously demonstrated to be interrelated to the relative success or failure of VLE engagement, that is, beliefs and expectations, computer self-efficacy, learning approaches and, finally, computer anxiety.

Each of these variables were assessed via similar research instruments; questionnaires which ranged in length (from 10 items measuring computer self-efficacy to 18 items used to assess the students approaches to learning) but which were each constructed with 11-point scales. Student participants therefore responded to the questionnaires by indicating the extent to which they agreed or disagreed with the statements provided in each questionnaire on a scale of 0–10.

The researchers utilized a sample of forty-two participants, half of which were drawn from a sociology course and a half from medical course. The results of an initial pretesting designed to elicit participant's computer skills and prior IT experience indicated that there was no significant difference between the two groups of students, and that they could thus be considered comparable in terms of their computer background. The questionnaires designed to elicit responses on each of the four variables were administered to the students both before and after they had attended the VLE-based course. The researchers aimed to establish whether or not the students had responded differently in these two (before and after conditions) and thus selected a test of difference for their analysis.

Choice of test

As all students (both medical and sociology) were included in both the before and after conditions, a related or within-groups test was required. As the data to be analysed were collected on an ordinal level of measurement (that is, that there is no guarantee of equidistance between the separate points on any of the 11-point scales used) a non-parametric test was chosen. Thus, the non-parametric test of difference for a two-condition within-groups design was the Wilcoxon signed ranks test.

Results

The results of the Wilcoxon testing indicated that for the most part, attending the VLE-based course appeared to have no significant impact on any of the variables under consideration. There was however one exception to this – whereas the students scores on the factors of beliefs and expectations, self-efficacy and learning approaches did not change between the before and after conditions for either group, it was found that scores on the final variable – computer anxiety – did change significantly, but that this was only in the case of the sociology students, who appeared to experience increased levels of computer anxiety following the course when compared to their levels prior to when the course began ($Z = -2.25$, $p < .05$). The medical students in contrast experienced no changes in anxiety levels between the before and after conditions.

The differences between the two groups of students have been more directly addressed in the section on Mann-Whitney, below.

Difference: between groups (the Mann-Whitney U-test)

This section outlines three studies on various aspects of the psychology of learning, each of which has employed the Mann-Whitney U-test. The first leads directly on from, and is indeed an extension of, the VLE study above. The second expands upon the treatment of VLE uptake by considering additional features of VLE use. The final study reported here steps back a little from these contemporary approaches to learning and teaching and draws on the behaviourist tradition in order to consider learning as a form of therapy, particularly with regard to procedures for 'unlearning' irrational fears.

1. Vuorela and Nummenmaa (2004)

Aims and methods

Vuorela and Nummenmaa (2004) cite previous work which suggests that among the most salient factors in students' successful use of learning technology are their own prior experiences of, and also their attitudes toward, the technology itself. Drawing on the theory of planned behaviour (Ajzen, 1991), the researchers describe students' attitudes toward a given behaviour – such as using a VLE – as their beliefs about the consequences of performing that behaviour (behavioural beliefs), and their evaluation of its consequences (outcome evaluations). Hence, students' beliefs about the consequences of using a VLE and their evaluation of those consequences are likely to affect their engagement with the VLE.

The researchers examined both behavioural beliefs and outcome evaluations of the students' engagement with the VLE technology by administering a questionnaire composed of a series of statements to which they responded along an 11-point scale, that is, from 0 (most negative belief and outcomes) to 10 (most positive beliefs and outcomes). This therefore represented the two dependent variables – of behavioural beliefs and outcome evaluations. These were considered to represent an ordinal scale, since there could be no guarantee that distances between the points on either scale would be equal. The independent variable for this part of their experiment was the students' domain of study, and for which there were two conditions – either medicine or sociology.

Choice of test

The design of this stage of the experiment was therefore unrelated, or between-groups (since the sociology students would obviously not be included within the same condition as the medical students) and the nature of the testing which would be required was a test of difference. As the data collected could not be considered to conform to parametric assumptions (as its level of measurement was ordinal), the most suitable test of difference for this two-condition, independent, non-parametric design was the Mann-Whitney.

Results

The Mann-Whitney test was administered twice for this part of the study – firstly prior to the course taking place, and secondly subsequent to its completion. The results of the test conducted prior to the onset of the course indicated that there were no significant differences in the behavioural beliefs and outcome evaluations between medical and sociology students. However, when the post-course test scores were analysed, a number of significant differences emerged. The medical students interpreted the learning environment more negatively than did the sociology students after the course, in terms of both behavioural beliefs ($U = 30.5$, $p < 0.01$) and outcome evaluations ($U = 59.00$, $p < 0.05$). This may support the notion that medical students are 'less at home' or more dissatisfied with technology than sociology students, although, as the researchers point out, further research would need to be undertaken to determine whether this is the case and if so then just why this should be so.

2. Lang and Lazovik (1963)

Aims and methods

Alongside that of approaches to teaching and learning, one of the longer lasting legacies of the behaviourist approach in psychology has been its application to the treatment of anxiety, most notably in terms of its desensitization of fears or phobias. One such study, which investigated the extent to which a desensitization procedure can influence the levels of fear in an organism (i.e. serve to decrease the levels of anxiety in a participant or patient) was that conducted by Lang and Lazovik (1963).

This study was based on an experimental design in which a number of students who had declared their fear of snakes undertook a two-stage therapy program based on training followed by desensitization. The training element was comprised of one-to-one sessions with a therapist where participants established a hierarchy of fear, that is, from the least fearful scenario such as just hearing the word 'snake', to the most fearful scenario such as actually holding one in their hands. Also incorporated within the training element were lessons in muscle relation, where the participants were instructed in deep muscle relaxation techniques which would be later used to try to offset their fear responses.

The desensitization element involved each participant working through their personal hierarchy of fear, each time attempting the deep muscle relation techniques they had acquired as part of the training element. They were required to take each part of the hierarchy step by step, so that no scenario could be addressed until the previous (i.e. lower on the hierarchy) scenario had been dealt with. In other words, the participants needed to demonstrate relaxation and ease with a given step before being allowed to move on to the next.

In design terms the independent variable of this study was the desensitization element itself. All participants received the training element, but only half received the desensitization element. In other words, the experimental subjects received desensitization therapy while the control subjects did not. The dependent variable was measured by making a direct observation of the subject behaviour when faced by a real-life snake. This was known as the snake avoidance test, and was based on a 19-point rating scale administered by the researcher, for example, from a top score of 1 where the subject held the snake, a score of 2 where the participant briefly touched the snake down to the base score of 19, where the subject refused to even enter the room. The higher the score attained by the participant, the stronger the avoidance of the snake.

Choice of test

As this snake avoidance test was comprised of points on a scale which cold not be guaranteed to be equidistant (i.e. the distance between points 1 and 2 could not be assumed to be exactly the same as the distance between points 18 and 19 on the scale) then the level of measurement of this dependent variable was assumed to be ordinal. In terms of the design considerations, this was clearly of a between-groups nature, with one group of participants being at one level of the independent variable (the experimental condition) and the other being at the second level (the control condition), and thus with clear independence from one another. In accordance with the unrelated design and the ordinal nature of the data, the Mann-Whitney U-test was used in order to test for significant differences between the two groups.

Results

The findings of the Mann-Whitney test indicated that there was a statistically significant difference between the individual change scores of all the experimental subjects when compared with all the control subjects ($p < 0.05$), in other words supporting the hypothesis that the exposure to the desensitization element of the study did indeed lead to a reduced level of anxiety or snake-phobia among the snake-phobic students.

3. Joiner, Brosnan, Duffield, Gavin and Maras (2007)

Aims and methods

As an example of the use of both the Mann-Whitney and the Spearman correlation coefficient (described below), we could consider the paper by Joiner et al. (2007) which takes as its focus the increasing importance of the internet to many everyday activities, including entertainment, communication and education. In particular, they concentrate on the internet's contribution to education. They stress that although it is acknowledged that changes in education are likely to mean that internet skills will become indispensable for lifelong learning, it appears that certain social groups continue to be under-represented in this area. Further, that such under-representation is not as a result of a lack of access but that it is more related to cognitive, motivational and affective factors.

Their research refers to two interrelated factors which have been shown to influence an individual's use of networked computing technology – of *internet* identification and *internet* anxiety. The former term can be understood as referring to self-definition, of how the internet user conceptualizes his or her own internet use as well as referring to identifying with others who share the same views and goals with respect to this aspect of information technology. The latter term can be defined as an irrational anticipation or fear evoked by the thought of using (or of actually using) the internet, resulting in avoiding or minimizing its use.

The perceived relationship of internet anxiety and internet use is that anything which increases a person's internet anxiety leads them to disidentify with any internet activities, and will then lead that person to form negative attitudes toward the technology – meaning that the individual is more likely to avoid activities, contexts and careers involving this aspect of IT. Specifically, the researchers tested the hypotheses that (1) internet anxiety will be inversely related to internet use, (2) internet identification will be positively related to internet use, and (3) internet identification will be inversely related to internet anxiety. Additionally, the researchers wished to determine any significant difference in use, identification and anxiety between the male and female participants.

Choice of test

The measures used to test the first three hypotheses were the number of hours per week participants spent on the internet, and questionnaire-derived scales for internet anxiety and internet identification – each comprised of questions rated on a 5-point Likert scale. The analytical approach used to test these three main hypotheses was that of correlation, as outlined in the section on the Spearman correlation coefficient below.

However, the approach used to determine *differences* on the above three measures of use – identification and anxiety between male and female participants – was based on the Mann-Whitney test. This is due to the orientation of this research question being one based on differences – that is, the question is aimed at uncovering any differences between groups (in this case of male and female internet users) rather than uncovering any association or correlation between the three measures. The Mann-Whitney was considered a suitable test of difference in this case due to the design, that is, that it would be testing differences between male and female participants, and also due to the level of measurement of the data (i.e. the ordinal nature of Likert measurements). Additionally, the researchers confirmed that initial analyses of the data indicated that the scale level variables (i.e. number of hours spent online) were all highly and positively skewed, and that they therefore chose to employ non-parametric statistics throughout the statistical analysis.

Results

In terms of the actual findings of the research, comparison of males and females via Mann-Whitney revealed significant differences for each prediction. In terms of internet identification, male identification with the internet was significantly higher than that of female identification ($Z = 2.3$, $p < 0.01$) and male participants were also significantly more likely to feel part of an internet community than were females ($Z = 3.1$, $p < 0.01$). The researchers also found men to be significantly less anxious about the internet than are their female counterparts ($Z = 3.6$, $p < 0.01$), adding to other findings which they feel suggests the internet to be a masculinized domain.

Correlation (the Spearman rank order correlation coefficient)

As in Section 4.1.3, where two tests of difference were followed by consideration of a test of correlation, we now turn our attention away from the Wilcoxon and Mann-Whitney to the Spearman rank order correlation coefficient (more often simply referred to as Spearman's rho). Two illustrations of the Spearman rho are therefore outlined below. The first continues the reporting of the Joiner et al. study above, with a switch in emphasis to considering the relationships between the internet related variables under study as opposed to the differences between the participants. The second example of the Spearman shows how it can be used as a validation method in the development of new research instruments. Just as the Pearson was shown to be utilized for such purposes in 4.1.3, so too can its non-parametric equivalent. For neatness and comparability purposes, this illustration also follows a similar theme in terms of the content being covered (i.e. assessment of drinking activity).

1. Joiner, Brosnan, Duffield, Gavin and Maras (2007)

Aims and methods

We can continue to refer to the above Joiner et al. study when considering our next test, the Spearman rank order correlation coefficient. Although the above Mann-Whitney analysis reflects the approach taken by the researchers to identify differences between groups, that is, the relationship between the male and female participants on the aforementioned variables, the other main aim of their research was to identify relationships between the variables themselves.

The hypotheses being tested referred to how internet anxiety related to internet use (as measured by the number of hours per week participants spent on the internet), how internet use related to internet identification (as measured by a questionnaire), and how internet identification related to internet anxiety (again, as measured by a questionnaire). The measures used to test the first three hypotheses were the number of hours per week participants spent on the internet, and questionnaire-derived scales for internet anxiety and internet identification – each comprised of questions rated on a 5-point Likert scale.

Choice of test

The reason underlying the choice of the Spearman to anaylse these three pairs of relationship was down to the level of measurement of the collected data. While internet use was assessed via a scale level of measurement (i.e. that of time – in this case the number of hours) the remaining two variables were both assessed via an ordinal level of measurement, that of 5-point Likert scales. For each of the three pair wise comparisons, then, the variables being tested were either scale-ordinal or ordinal-ordinal. In other words there was no testing for significant correlations for scale-scale variables, and therefore the Pearson correlation coefficient was not considered suitable.

Results

The results of the Spearman testing reveled a number of significant relationships; the researcher found that internet identification was positively related to internet use both in terms of general internet use ($p = 0.49$, $p < 0.01$) and in using the internet for coursework ($p = 0.20$, $p < 0.01$). There was, conversely, a significant and negative relationship between internet identification and internet anxiety ($p = -0.14$, $p < 0.01$). There was also found to be a significant negative relationship between internet anxiety and general internet use ($p = -0.17$, $p < 0.05$) although anxiety was neither negatively nor positively related to the use of the internet for coursework.

In summary then, the results indicated a positive relationship between internet identification and use, a negative relationship between internet identification and anxiety and a negative relationship between internet anxiety and use. On the whole then, most students were not anxious about using the internet, although those who were more anxious about using the internet used the internet less. Those who scored high on internet identification used the internet more than those who did not. Incidentally, the authors acknowledge the limitations of the study in that, as with all correlation, it is not possible to draw causal links between variables; for example, it is possible that a person's strong identification with the internet caused them to use the internet more, but it is just as likely that the students may have identified more with the internet simply because of their frequent use of it.

2. Young, Hasking, Oeic and Loveday (2007)

Aims and methods

The second illustration of the use of the Spearman correlation coefficient departs from the learning and teaching theme to return to the other student activity mentioned earlier (Windle 2004), and considers the paper by Young et al. (2007). The experiment reported therein covers similar ground in terms of the subject matter (alcohol consumption), but also, just as with the Windle study, the research by Young et al. is oriented toward the validation of a research instrument rather than purely to the analysis of data to provide evidence to support a particular hypothesis.

The researchers here claim that, although excessive drinking among young people and adolescents is recognized as a concern, there are relatively few valid psychometric tools designed for such groups. Their research therefore aims to refine and adapt an existing tool in this area – The Drinking Refusal Self-Efficacy Questionnaire (DRSEQ) – which was designed to assess an individual's belief in their ability to resist drinking alcohol.

Central to their research is the concept of self-efficacy, the belief that one is capable of performing in a certain manner to attain certain goals. The original DRSEQ consists of three factors reflecting three particular variations of self-efficacy. These have been classed as social pressure refusal self-efficacy, opportunistic refusal self-efficacy and emotional relief refusal self-efficacy. The DRSEQ requires that on each of these factors, participants should rate the included statements on a 6-point Likert scale, with higher scores indicating a higher level of refusal self-efficacy. In addition to that produced by the questionnaires, data were also collected on the actual alcohol consumption of participants, in terms of the total volume per week and number of days per week in which alcohol was consumed.

Choice of test

As the questionnaire data, being based on Likert scales, were clearly of an ordinal level of measurement, the researchers chose the Spearman over the Pearson correlation coefficient. This choice was further supported when the consumption measures, which were by their nature considered as a scale level of measurement, were examined and found to be all positively skewed. The consumption measures therefore failed to fulfil the further parametric requirement that scores (even on a scale level of measurement) should be normally distributed. Spearman's rho was therefore chosen to determine the extent of the correlations between the DRSEQ (both total and subscale scores) and the extent of alcohol consumption.

Results

The findings indicated that all subscales of the DRSEQ, as well as the total score, were negatively correlated with average alcohol consumption per week. This was in terms of both the number of days on which alcohol was consumed each week (total DRSEQ score by days ($r = -.37$, $p < 0.001$)) and the total volume actually consumed (total DRSEQ score by volume ($r = -.36$, $p < 0.001$)). Overall, the results of these analyses were accepted as support for the robust three-factor structure underlying the DRSEQ, enabling the use of the research instrument to be extended from clinical and adult applications to adolescent samples.

NON-PARAMETRIC TESTING (ORDINAL) 165

4.2.4 Narrative

Just as in the previous section, where we considered the continuing research investigation into Friday morning alertness via parametric tests, we should – with a little variation in the research design and data being collected – be able to see how non-parametric tests can also be used within such a scenario. The simplest way to approach this would be to replicate the treatment given to the reaction time study in 4.1.4, only this time using the non-parametric equivalents to the t-tests and Pearson correlation coefficient. This section will thus demonstrate how the application of the Mann-Whitney, Wilcoxon signed ranks and Spearman's rho can contribute to the Friday morning feeling study.

Difference: between groups (the Mann-Whitney test)

Way back in Section 1.1.4, we looked into the possibility of comparing the reaction time scores of two groups of individuals via their ranked scores as opposed to their actual reaction times as measured in milliseconds – this being the Week 2 experiment, where an apparent fault in the reaction time program meant that the accuracy of the readings given in ms could not be confirmed. So as not to abandon the experiment, the order in which the participants completed the task – who came first, second, third etc. – was noted and used as the basis of the analysis rather than the actual millisecond recordings. This resulting dataset was therefore composed of ranks, considered to represent an ordinal level of measurement due to there being no guarantee of the distances between them being the same. As the data were ordinal, and the experimental design was to investigate differences between two groups, the Mann-Whitney would be the selected test to achieve this – with typical SPSS outputs being as in Tables 4.20 and 4.21.

(The results of the analysis could thus be expressed as $U = 23$, $N_1 = 10$, $N_2 = 10$, $p = 0.04$ [2-tailed]).

Table 4.20 illustrates the mean ranks of the two conditions, with the non-clubbing group clearly demonstrating the faster reaction times (as the lower the numerical rank represents the faster the time of completion, as in 1 for fastest, 2 for second fastest and so on).

Table 4.20 Mann-Whitney ranks

	Activity	N	Mean rank	Sum of ranks
RT_Position	Clubbing	10	13.20	132.00
	Non-clubbing	10	7.80	78.00
	Total	20		

Table 4.21 Mann-Whitney statistics[a]

	RT_Position
Mann-Whitney U	23.000
Wilcoxon W	78.000
Z	−2.041
Asymp. Sig. (2-tailed)	.041
Exact Sig. [2*(1-tailed Sig.)]	.043[b]

[a] Grouping variable: activity.
[b] Not corrected for ties.

Table 4.21 includes the inferential results which tell us whether or not this difference is significant. As can be seen here, the difference in the mean ranks between the clubbers and non-clubbers is actually significant, with a p value of 0.04, thus lending support for the notion that once again Thursday nights out do tend to affect Friday morning reaction times.

Difference: within groups (the Wilcoxon test)

If we progress our non-parametric treatment of the reaction time/ alertness experiment to a within participant design, we can perhaps conceptualize the above ranking procedure as being applied to the Week 4 and Week 5 scenario first outlined in Section 1.2.4. Here, we saw the researcher collecting reaction time data from the group of students who had been partaking of the local nightlife the previous evening, and then again with the very same group of students being invited along for the reaction time experiment of the following week – only with the second data collection taking place following a Thursday night spent at home watching TV. Thus, the same students of the 'night out' condition from Week 4 also represented the 'night in' condition of Week 5.

The original level of measurement used and described in Section 1.2.4 was scale, that is, reaction times recorded in milliseconds. However, in the event of a program malfunction occurring here, just as it had done in Week 2 (which we've just covered as part of the Munn-Whitney example above), then the researcher could once again use ranks instead of actual reaction time values. In other words, he could compare the relative positions of the participants for the night out condition of Week 4 with the position of those same participants for the night in condition of Week 5. In order to achieve this, he would most likely use the Wilcoxon signed ranks test – the test most suited to determining any significant difference between two conditions when data is of an ordinal level of measurement. Typical SPSS outputs are included in Tables 4.22 and 4.23.

(The results of the analysis could thus be expressed as $Z = -0.06$, $N = 10$, $p = 0.95$ [2-tailed]).

The above figures show us the mean ranks (in Table 4.22) and also the results of the inferential test (Table 4.23). The former

Table 4.22 Wilcoxon ranks

		N	Mean rank	Sum of ranks
Non-clubbing – Clubbing	Negative ranks	5[a]	4.40	22.00
	Positive ranks	4[b]	5.75	23.00
	Ties	1[c]		
	Total	10		

[a] Non-clubbing < Clubbing.
[b] Non-clubbing > Clubbing.
[c] Non-clubbing = Clubbing.

Table 4.23 Wilcoxon statistics[a]

	Non-clubbing – Clubbing
Z	-.061[b]
Asymp. Sig. (2-tailed)	.951

[a] Wilcoxon signed ranks test.
[b] Based on negative ranks.

shows us that the number of participants who were faster in the clubbing condition (four) almost equaled the number who were faster in the non-clubbing condition (five) with one participant holding the same ranked position on each occasion. The latter table indicates whether or not this difference is significant. In this case, the difference in the mean ranks between the clubbing and non-clubbing condition, with a p value of 0.95, is clearly not statistically significant.

This is perhaps not entirely surprising, as it reflects the nature of the test – that is, that the test considers rank order, and that an individual who was the fastest of a group of participants in one condition is also likely to be the fastest in another condition (providing that all other participants received the same treatment) even though the actual reaction time in milliseconds may be very different. This perhaps highlights one of the considerations which should be made before attempting to use tests of ordinal data for within participant research designs.

Correlation (the Spearman rank order correlation coefficient)

Our third and final consideration of the Thursday/Friday alertness study from an ordinal data perspective involves the use of the Spearman rank order correlation coefficient.

Let's consider that after all these weeks of Thursday night activity followed by Friday morning data collection, our intrepid researcher begins to become a little concerned with the student's perception of the experiment, that they just might be getting a bit cheesed off with the whole thing. In order to put his mind at rest – and to also throw another variable into the equation and thus the chance to write a paper for another conference on a completely different angle – he asks the participants to complete a questionnaire after the reaction time program has been completed. This questionnaire attempts to elicit the impressions which the students have of the experiment by asking them to rate various aspects on a 1 to 7 scale. The researcher then calculates the median score of these responses to demonstrate that the participants were actually quite enjoying the experience. However, the questionnaire data could also be used alongside the reaction time results in order to see if there was any relationship between the two – that is, would fast reaction times be associated with high ratings, or vice versa.

This would therefore form the basis for an analysis using the Spearman correlation coefficient. By using the fastest to slowest rankings data outlined in the previous scenario in conjunction with the ratings derived from the questionnaire, the researcher would have two variables based on an ordinal level of measurement. To determine any significant relationship between the two, the researcher would need to examine the outputs of the Spearman test, as per the examples (Figure 4.4 and Table 4.24).

(The results of the analysis could thus be expressed as $p = .93$, $N = 10$, $p < 0.001$ [2-tailed]).

As with the Pearson coefficient detailed earlier, the output of the Spearman takes the form of a 'mirrored' table, with each result appearing twice. Essentially, the table (Table 4.24) gives us the value of Spearman's rho, and also the significance of this figure. In this case, the value of the coefficient is positive and extremely high, at .93, indicating a potentially very strong correlation between the two variables. This is reinforced with the p value given, of $p < 0.001$.

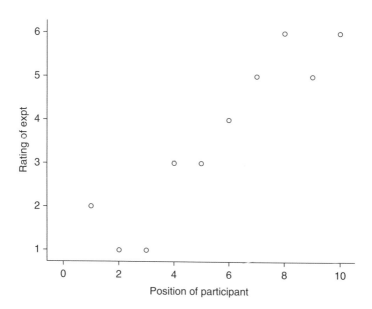

Figure 4.4 Scatter plot of the relationship between experiment ratings and ranked position

Table 4.24 Results of the Spearman correlation coefficient

			Rating of expt	Position of participant
Spearman's rho	Rating of Expt	Correlation coefficient	1.000	.926**
		Sig. (2-tailed)		.000
		N	10	10
	Position of participant	Correlation coefficient	.926**	1.000
		Sig. (2-tailed)	.000	
		N	10	10

** Correlation is significant at the 0.01 level (2-tailed).

4.2.5 Further reading

Field, A. P. (2005). *Discovering Statistics Using SPSS (and Sex, Drugs and Rock 'n' Roll)* 2nd Edition. Sage. sections 13.2, 13.3.

Brace, N., Kemp, R. and Snelgar, R. (2009). *SPSS for Psychologists 4th Edition*. Palgrave Macmillan. chapter 3, sections 5 & 6 and chapter 4, section 4.

Howitt, D. and Cramer, D. (2008). *Introduction to SPSS in Psychology 4th Edition*. Pearson Prentice Hall. chapter 14.

Howitt, D. and Cramer, D. (2008). *Introduction to Statistics in Psychology 4th Edition*. Pearson Prentice Hall. chapter 18.

4.3 Non-parametric testing (nominal)

The final section of this chapter on inferential statistics – and indeed the final major section of the book – deals with the analysis of data collected at the most basic level of measurement, that of nominal or categorical data. As with the previous two sections, it describes the non-parametric tests to be used when investigating the differences between groups and also the differences within groups, via the chi square and McNemar tests respectively. In each case, the test is covered in terms of the assumptions upon which they are based, everyday illustrations of their use and also representative examples from the psychological literature. However, unlike the previous sections, there is no nominal data correlation test covered here. Although such a test -known as the Phi coefficient – does exist, its use is so rare in psychological research that (and in accordance with most other texts) it has not been included here.

4.3.1 Concepts

Difference: between groups (the chi square test)

When we have collected data which cannot be ranked or ordered and can only be counted or categorized, then we need to use a test designed for a nominal level of measurement. When the data has been collected via a between groups design, we would normally choose the chi square test.

The chi square test compares actual observations, or numbers of instances, with the number of instances which would be expected by chance alone. In its simplest form, it is represented as a 2 × 2 table or grid, the grid being referred to in this way as it cross-tabulates two variables, each with two possible (and mutually exclusive) values. It is in this simplest format that we shall consider the chi square here. It should also be noted that the chi square test can be considered as a test of difference and also as a test of association (as outlined in the example below). The use of this chi square test is thus applicable in situations where:

- The data are held in two variables, each with mutually exclusive categories
- The data in both variables are measured on a nominal level of measurement
- The participants counted in the first category are not also counted in the second category

Difference: within groups (the McNemar test)

There are a number of within-groups tests equivalent to the chi square, although these are not encountered as often in psychological research studies as the chi square itself. One of the most useful is the McNemar test, which is something of a 'cut down' version of the chi square, in that it just addresses two categories, each relating to the same participants. The use of the McNemar test is thus applicable in situations where:

- The data are held in one variable, which has two mutually exclusive categories
- The data in both variables is measured on a nominal level of measurement
- The participants counted in the first category are also counted in the second category

4.3.2 Everyday examples

Difference: between groups (the chi square test)

Everyday examples of the findings of chi square results (or perhaps findings that *should* have been produced via chi square testing, rather) can frequently be found whenever claims are made of how certain numbers of people differ in their views, attitudes or decision-making. The property-oriented TV shows which we

encountered earlier in Section 4.2.2 often talk of how first time
buyers are less likely than non-first time buyers to take out a mort-
gage in times of recession, while political reports on the evening
news frequently state findings such as how northerners and south-
erners differ in their left/right wing voting intentions, or of how
more Londoners object to the principle of the congestion charge
than do non-Londoners (for rather obvious reasons). We might
also see more lighthearted items claiming that more women than
men opt for watching Strictly as opposed to the X Factor, or maybe
of how more students than non-students watch Dr Who on a
Saturday night rather than watch whatever else is on. Even an offbeat example such as how children and adults differ in their belief
of Santa Claus would fit into the chi square template.

In fact, each of these examples can be thought of as a 2 × 2
grid, with the rows and columns representing mutually exclusive categories. The four numerical cells of each table represent the numbers of individuals corresponding to each of these
categories – with the golden chi square rule that it is not possible for any given individual to be counted in more than one cell
in each table. Sample grids of the two aforementioned examples, using hypothetical data, are included in Table 4.25.

The chi square test: typical SPSS outputs

If we take the aforementioned and rather whimsical notion of the
existence of a supernatural yuletide entity as the basis of our first
SPSS illustration, we can see how the typical output would appear.

Table 4.26 in the output reflects pretty much that which we already
know, that is, the numbers of cases which can be classed as belong-
ing to each of the four categories, and also with the totals of the
rows and columns – total number of adults and children, and total
numbers of believers and non-believers. Perhaps the most surprising

Table 4.25 Sample 2 × 2 chi square grids

		Belief in Santa					Saturday viewing	
		Yes	No				Dr Who	Who knows?
Age	Child	38	16		Status	Student	48	18
	Adult	6	40			Non-student	14	20

aspect of the results within this first table is that, out of a total of forty-six adults, six of them apparently are still keeping the faith.

However, as delightful as this may sound, the results in Table 4.27 suggest that these half a dozen are actually quite the exception, and that there is indeed a statistically significant difference in the number of adults believing in Santa as compared to the number of children who are still convinced, as indicated by the large chi square value of 33.13 and the p value of less than 0.001. We may therefore also say that there is an association between these two variables – of age and belief in Santa – with children

Table 4.26 Cross-tabs of belief in Santa by age

		Santa		Total
		Believes	Doesn't believe	
Age	Child	38	16	54
	Adult	6	40	46
Total		44	56	100

Table 4.27 Chi square statistic for belief in Santa by age

	Value	df	Asymp. sig. (2-sided)	Exact sig. (2-sided)	Exact sig. (1-sided)
Pearson chi-square	33.130[a]	1	.000		
Continuity correction[b]	30.845	1	.000		
Likelihood ratio	35.932	1	.000		
Fisher's exact test				.000	.000
Linear-by-linear association	32.799	1	.000		
N of valid cases	100				

[a] 0 cells (.0%) have expected count less than 5. The minimum expected count is 20. 24.
[b] Computed only for a 2 × 2 table.

being significantly more likely than adults to be listening out for the sound of sleigh bells on Christmas Eve.

(The results of the analysis could thus be expressed as $x^2 = 33.13$, df = 1, p < 0.001 [2-tailed]).

Difference: within groups (the McNemar test)

Similar examples can be found around us of the findings of studies appearing to have used a nominal within-groups design. For instance, the number of people who thought watching Big Brother was a good idea when the first series was first shown compared to those who still thought it was a good idea by the time series 10 graced our screens would fall into this category. Similarly, the number of Londoners driving 4 × 4s before the introduction of the congestion charge who were still driving that model one year after the charge had been in force would also represent the within-groups nominal design. Other examples could include the number of people intending to cast their vote in an election before as compared to after the expenses scandal rose to prominence, or even of the number of people willing to trust the banks with their savings before and after the onset of the credit crunch. In all these cases, the dependent variable consists of the number of people or respondents in each category. The essential difference between these and the previous chi square examples is that they involve the same groups of people in both the (before and after) conditions.

The McNemar test: typical SPSS outputs

Let's consider a relatively simple nominal data-based scenario, based on our perhaps familiar experience of political opinion polls. We tend to hear of these often, with the results of the latest polls of the relative Labour-Liberal-Conservative support being revealed on almost a daily basis. They do also seem to receive particular attention on Thursday nights for some reason? During the approach to local or general elections they become even more visible – so they are certainly something to which we can probably relate.

However, in this case, let's say a researcher is interested in a little more than simple opinion polls and aims to shed some light on what actually helps to form those opinions in the first place. She forms a hypothesis that political views are firmly entrenched within us and are not easily influenced – certainly not by the party political broadcasts (PPBs) that invade our TV viewing as we approach election time. She thus proposes the null hypothesis and experimental hypotheses, that

- H_0 there will be no statistically significant difference in the number of voters planning to vote for 'Party A' before that party's PPB compared to after that party's PPB.
- H_1 there will be a statistically significant difference in the number of voters planning to vote for 'Party A' before that party's PPB compared to after that party's PPB.

The above suggests a potential 2 × 2 chi square scenario of 'seen/ not seen PPB'and 'changed/not changed mind'. In other words, we could consider those who had seen/had not seen, the PPB and also those who had changed their minds/not changed their minds. However, this could be simplified to some extent, just by focusing on the participants who *had* actually seen the PPB. This could still be interpreted as a 2 × 2 grid, but in this case – because the study included just those who *had* seen the PPB – it would be considered a within groups design.

Let's say that the PPB is scheduled for a Tuesday night (let's give Thursdays a break!), so the researcher asks the simple question of 'will you vote for Party A?' on the Monday and again asks the same question on the Wednesday. By using this simpler approach we will thus have two conditions where each elicits nominal level data (a simple Yes or No) either side of an intervention (the PPB itself). Assuming a sample size of a hundred voters, the resulting grid may look something like Table 4.28, cross-tabulating the 'will vote' and 'won't vote' responses with the before and after conditions.

(The results of the analysis could thus be expressed as McNemar $x^2 = 0.46$, N = 100, p = 0.50 [2-tailed]).

In considering Tables 4.28 and 4.29, we can see that there were indeed some change in voting intention following the broadcast. We can see that 35 of the 100 participants experienced a change of heart following the broadcast. However, as this change took place in both directions (20 in the direction of voting, 15 in the direction of *not* voting), the overall effect may be less than initially thought. This is confirmed by the results which indicate that the changes recorded in voters responses between either side of the PPB were,

Table 4.28 Cross-tabs of voting intention before PPB by after PPB

	After	
Before	Not vote	Will vote
Not vote	35	20
Will vote	15	30

Table 4.29 Statistics of voting intention before PPB by after PPB[a]

	Before and After
N	100
Chi square[b]	.457
Asymp. sig.	.499

[a] McNemar test.
[b] Continuity corrected.

with a p value of 0.50, not statistically significant. We can therefore conclude that, as the researcher suspected, the PPB had no overall impact on voting intentions (and thus the null in this case is not rejected).

4.3.3 From the literature

Difference: between groups (the chi square test)

As with the previous 'from the literature sections' there follow a number of synopses of actual studies which have been conducted by psychologists – in this case two of recent origin and one dating back to the sixties – and which have used the chi square test in the analyses of the collected data. In this section, the case studies are drawn from three quite diverse areas. The first concerns a field experiment on patterns of pro-social behaviour undertaken in order to uncover the reactions of bystanders in public places to potential emergency situations. The second study concerns the contemporary issue of mobile phone usage, and of eliciting the attitudes of mobile users toward the content of what actually appears on their gadgets. The third and final study considers various implications of one of the topics that appears throughout this book – that of eating and drinking.

1. Piliavin, Rodin and Piliavin (1969)

Aims and methods

Perhaps one of the most famous psychological experiments to be outlined within this book for the purposes of illustrating the use of statistical tests, and one which we have already encountered back in the first chapter, is that conducted by Piliavin et al. (1969). This took the form of a field experiment, undertaken in order to investigate the effects of a number of factors influencing helping behaviour in a public setting. The setting in question was an underground train on the New York subway system – hence the unofficial reference to the location of this study as being 'a laboratory on wheels'. The factors, or independent variables, which were investigated in this study included physical appearance, race, sex and physical proximity – all being manipulated in order to gauge their effect on the likelihood of a member of the public coming to the aid of someone apparently in need of assistance.

The procedure for the study involved four teams of students each being made up of three members, that is, a model or 'victim', and two observers. Each team staged standard collapse scenarios on the subway train in which the victim feigned illness. The variations in each scenario, and hence the manipulation of the independent variables, included physical appearance of the victim (i.e. appearing to be either drunk or ill), and also the race of the victim (black or white).

The data that were recorded by the observers included the actual number of bystanders coming to the aid of the potentially injured party, and also their sex, race, speed of response and physical distance from the victim. The factors of sex and race clearly represent a nominal level of measurement (i.e. male or female, black or white), while the factor of speed of response or 'latency' was modified such that this too was considered to be a nominal level of measurement (the recorded response times of the bystanders were collapsed into two categories, fast and slow).

Choice of test

The staged collapses focusing on each of the above variations were performed at different times and with different members of the public present on each occasion. In terms of the research design then, the field experiment was considered as being unrelated as it was assumed that no bystanders would be present in more than one condition. When considering the between-groups nature of the research design, and the nominal level of measurement of many of the aforementioned variables (appearance, race, sex, latency categorization), the researchers chose the chi square test as the most suitable analytical procedure to analyse the collected data.

Results

It is often the case that chi square analyses and their subsequent findings are more clearly interpreted via reference to a cross-tabulation table. The two tables making up Table 4.30 are therefore used to illustrate the design and results of just two predictions made by the researchers conducting this study, that is, that the physical appearance of the victim (either drunk or genuinely ill) will affect the speed of response of the helper, and that the race of the victim (either white or black) will influence the behaviour of the helper dependent upon the helper's own race (either white or black).

The first table indicates that there was more immediate assistance being offered to the victims who appeared to be ill than those appearing to be intoxicated. This was confirmed via the chi square test ($x^2 = 36.83$, df = 2, p<0.001).

Table 4.30 The number of trials where help was offered before and after 70 seconds

		Time of response				Race of helper	
		Up to 70s	After 70s			Same	Different
Looks	Unwell	52	5	**Looks**	Unwell	36	26
	Drunk	5	19		Drunk	16	3

The second table, however, suggests the absence of a race effect in the helping behaviour. Despite the finding that more help was given by those of the same race as the victim, this was not found to be statistically significant, and the tendency to help ill victims rather than drunk victims remained regardless of race. The chi square results ($x^2 = 3.26$, $p = 0.08$) thus confirmed there to be no statistically significant effect of 'same race' helping.

The above results therefore suggest that firstly an (apparently) ill person is more likely to receive aid than is one who appears to be drunk, and secondly that the race of victim has little effect on the helping actions of members of the public as regards their own race. One further finding of the research, incidentally, was that male bystanders were significantly more likely to offer assistance than females ($x^2 = 30.63$, $p < .001$). Piliavin et al. found that although male bystanders accounted for just 60% of the people in the critical area, they accounted for *90%* of those offering help.

2. Tsang, Ho and Liang (2004)

Aims and methods

Although psychological studies aimed at determining participants views or attitudes toward a particular topic are very often associated with tests such as Wilcoxon and Mann-Whitney (due to the frequently found ordinal data of Likert-type attitude scales), many such investigations also make use of procedures designed to analyse data at a nominal level of measurement. Tsang et al. (2004) conducted one such study, eliciting people's views on, and attitudes toward, the changing nature of product advertising, with a particular focus on the use of the medium of mobile phones and mobile phone messaging for this purpose.

The study cites the ongoing revolution in information technology and the rapid proliferation of mobile phones and other mobile devices as providing new marketing channels and hence new opportunities for advertisers. Indeed, they claim that the use of texting to enable access to customers through their own mobile phones will increase markedly in the coming years, and that the mobile may well become the ultimate one-to-one marketing tool.

The (perhaps obvious) question to be asked here is how will mobile users respond to this increase? As another worthwhile feature to be added to the growing list of mobile phone capabilities, or simply as a gross invasion of privacy? To examine the potential user reaction, Tsang et al. (2004) investigated the phenomenon of consumer attitudes toward mobile advertising. Drawing on the theory of reasoned action (TRA) proposed by Fishbein and Ajzen, they examined the three major constructs of attitude (in this instance the attitude toward text-based ads), intention (to view text-based ads), and behaviour (to actually read these ads within a set time frame). The attitude component was measured via the use of a questionnaire designed specifically to collect data regarding consumer views on internet and mobile advertising. Additional questions were incorporated to assess intention via a scale of 'willingness' to receive text-based ads, and actual behaviour via estimates of the timing for reading the message – ranging from immediately reading it to completely ignoring it.

Among the hypotheses generated for the experiment were two which will be considered here; firstly, that providing incentives for receiving text-based ads significantly impacts consumer intentions to receive them, and secondly that consumers' intentions to receive mobile ads affect their behavior after the messages have been received. In other words, the researchers were looking at the relationship between attitude and intention, and the relationship between intention and behaviour.

When the analysis considered participant behaviour following the receiving of a mobile advert, they once again focused upon categorical data only this time in a larger grid. Instead of a 2 × 2 grid as with the first hypothesis the categories this time were such that a 2 × 4 grid was used (Table 4.31).

Table 4.31   Participant behaviour following receipt of mobile ads

		Timing of message reading			
		Ignore	Cumulate	Get later	Immediate
Intent	No	70	3	48	86
	Yes	11	0	33	85

Behaviour was measured in this instance by the extent to which an ad would be read in terms of the above four categories, ranging from immediately reading it to ignoring it.

Choice of test

The chi square test was chosen to test the hypothesis as firstly, data were categorical and mutually exclusive, and secondly as the design was unrelated. In examining the first prediction, the respondents were asked about their willingness to receive mobile advertising if certain rewards, such as free telephone time, were provided. Their responses were collapsed into four categories, that is, of 'yes with reward', 'yes regardless of reward', 'no with reward', and 'no regardless of reward'. As no participant could be included in more than one of these four categories, the design was considered to be between-groups. Thus, testing for differences in categorical data for a between-groups framework led to the choice of the chi square test being made.

Results

For the first hypothesis, a chi square test of the responses demonstrated that the effect of providing incentives was statistically significant at $p < 0.001$ ($x2 = 43.8$, $p < 0.001$). Hence the researchers accepted this as support for the first of the hypotheses above, that providing incentives can increase one's intention to receive text-based mobile adverts. For the second hypothesis, respondents who were willing to receive mobile ads tended to read the messages immediately, but those whose intention was not to receive mobile ads tended to ignore and not read the received messages ($x^2 = 57.43$, $p < 0.001$).

From the above chi square results, the researchers concluded that intention is affected by the incentive associated with the ad, that is, that the respondents were more willing to accept incentive-based mobile advertising. Additionally, they interpreted the results as support for the prediction that intention significantly affects how and when the respondents read the message, adding that advertisers may use the findings to design marketing programs with mobile ads that create positive attitudes and which provide incentives for engagement.

3. Matthews (2004)

Aims and methods

A number of earlier illustrations (i.e. the studies conducted by Windle 2004 and Young et al. 2007) have dealt with the analysis of data to determine relationships between drinking activity and psychological factors such as self-efficacy, primarily via correlational measures. However, such topics are of course not confined to the use of the Pearson or Spearman correlation coefficients. The data produced by such studies could be equally suited to the use of the chi square as the means of analysis, as was the case with the two part study undertaken by Matthews (2004), which examined the relationship between drinking deemed to be excessive or 'problematic' and eating patterns deemed to be extreme or 'disordered' among university students.

The first stage of the Matthews (2004) study was concerned with determining any sex differences in these areas of problem drinking and eating disorder (i.e. a comparison of male and female participants). The second stage of the study, however, focused specifically on the women in the study and thus sought to examine more closely any relationship between problem drinking and eating disorders among female students.

The participants in the study (N = 289, Male 64, Female 225) completed two standardized questionnaires, the Alcohol Use Disorders Identification Test (AUDIT) and the Eating Disorders Inventory (EDI2). The responses of the participants to each of these questionnaires were used to establish an individual alcohol use and eating pattern profile for each student. These resultant profiles were then categorized into dichotomous eating and drinking classifications, that is, of 'problem drinking', 'non-problem drinking', 'eating disorder' and 'non-eating disorder'. The numbers of participants corresponding to each of these categories was then counted.

Choice of test

The data analysis procedures, then, involved the initial scores on the questionnaires being processed and collapsed into the above categories, thus representing nominal data. As the research questions were oriented toward examining differences between men and women in the first instance, and differences between separate categories of women in the second instance, the design of both parts of the study could be considered as between groups. No participant would be in more than one condition or category; that is, either male or female, either 'eating disorder' or 'non-eating disorder' and so on. In view of the above, the researchers therefore chose a between-groups test of difference suitable for data that are collected on a nominal level of measurement – they therefore chose the chi square test as the basis for their inferential analysis.

Results

Results of the first stage of the study, testing for any significant differences between men and women in relation to rates of problem drinking and abnormal eating behaviour indicated that there was indeed a significant gender effect with the male participants being statistically more likely to engage in and to report problem drinking behaviour ($x^2 = 5.027$, df = 1, p = 0.025). Additionally, the chi square testing also found that the women in the study were significantly more likely to engage in and to report behaviours defined as eating disorders ($x^2 = 7.392$, df = 1, p = 0.007).

Table 4.32 Cross-tabs of Sex × Drinking, Sex × Eating and Eating × Drinking

		Sex	
		Male	Female
Drink	Yes	17.2%	7.1%
	No	82.8%	92.9%

		Sex	
		Male	Female
Eat	Yes	6.3%	21.4%
	No	93.7%	78.6%

		Eating	
		Yes	No
Drink	Yes	3.1%	8.9%
	No	17.8%	70.2%

These findings (Table 4.32) were just as predicted by the researchers, and indeed were consistent with that of the existing literature in the area, that proportionately more men score positively for problem drinking while a higher percentage of women score positively for eating disorders.

The second stage of the study addressed only women (N = 225) and used the chi square to test for whether there was a significant positive relationship between those who score positively on the aforementioned research instrument for problem drinking and those who scored positively on that for eating disorders. The results of the test in this instance showed no such significant effect (x^2 = 0.471, df = 1, p = 0.492), supporting the view that there is no statistically significant association between problem drinking and problem eating among the women of the sample.

Difference: within groups (the McNemar test)

The final set of illustrations of this chapter deal with the within-groups equivalent of the chi square test, that is, the McNemar test. This tends to be used much less frequently in psychological studies than the chi square – and thus tends to be covered to a relatively lesser degree in many statistics texts (although see Brace et al. 2009 for a concise but very useful account of the test). Despite the relative lack of coverage, the McNemar is a very useful tool when examining 'before and after' effects, as seen in the following two scenarios. The first of these once again revisits the topic of eating, this time seeking to establish the effects of an intervention designed to improve self-esteem and discourage problem eating, while the second considers the increasingly popular phenomenon of social networking, and asks a number of interesting questions about the morality and ethics of online activity, considering these within the contexts of how such activities would be perceived in the real (i.e. non-online) world.

1. O'Dea and Abraham (2000)

Aims and methods

Our first example of the use of the McNemar test continues the theme of eating, this time with a focus upon its relationship with self-esteem and body image. O'Dea and Abraham (2000) examined the effect of an interactive, school-based education programme aimed at improving each students own body image by building general self-esteem in order to foster a positive sense of self, thereby discouraging the onset of eating disorders.

The researchers established a sample of 470 schoolchildren with an age range of 11–14, selected from two separate schools. These children were randomly allocated into an experimental, or 'intervention' group and a control group. The intervention group students participated in the program, whereas the control group students received their scheduled personal development and health class as normal – although the education program was made available to the students in the control group after the completion of the study.

To assess the impact of the intervention, all participants completed a number of questionnaires on three separate occasions. These were at the onset of the study (termed as baseline), once again after a three-month period and finally after twelve months had passed. The participants were also asked to indicate at each of these three points in time whether or not they were attempting to lose weight. It is this last measure – based on a simple dichotomous 'yes' or 'no' response – which comprised the data used for the McNemar test.

Choice of test

The McNemar test was chosen not only because of the nominal level of measurement, but also because the researchers aimed to test for differences taking place over time within the same group of participants, that is, to determine if there was any significant difference in the number of intervention group students attempting to lose weight at each of these three points in time, and similarly to determine if there was any difference in the number of control group students attempting to lose weight in the same periods. The comparison was therefore considered to be based on a within-groups design, as the first comparison (i.e. or the intervention group) involved the same participants in each of the three conditions, and similarly the second comparison (i.e. of the control group) also involved the same control participants in the three conditions.

Results

O'Dea and Abraham found that, although there were no significant differences between the number of students overall who reported currently trying to lose weight at baseline and at three and twelve months, this was not the case for the female students alone, where a number of significant changes were found. The researchers found that the number of female students in the control group who reported currently trying to lose weight increased significantly by 8% after the first three months (McNemar $x^2 = 3.85$, df = 1, p < .05), while the number of female students in the intervention group who reported currently trying to lose weight during the same period did not increase significantly (McNemar $x^2 = 0.38$, df = 1, p > .05).

However, this trend appeared to reverse by the time of the final data collection point, at twelve months from the study's commencement. The number of female students in the intervention group who reported currently trying to lose weight increased significantly by 9.0% at the twelve-month point (McNemar $x^2 = 6.42$, df = 1, p < .05), but the increase of 6% over 12 months in the female control group was found to be not statistically significant (McNemar $x^2 = 1.69$, df = 1, p > .05).

2. Foulger, Ewbank, Kay, Popp and Carter (2009)

Aims and methods

Our final illustration of the use of the McNemar test considers the use of social networking sites such as MySpace and Facebook. These are obviously very well known to the majority of students as informal means of communication, message (and photo) posting and just as a way of keeping in the loop. A paper by Foulger et al. (2009), however, focuses upon these as innovative digital tools which open up not just new networking and communication possibilities, but which may be changing the way in which we interact, and furthermore changing the ways in which we view the actual boundaries of interaction. They propose that traditional ideas of privacy and personal space are not yet well defined in the online world, citing a number of court cases where users have overstepped the mark and have been found somewhat wanting as regards the respect and responsibility which would have been afforded friends and colleagues in the traditional non-online world. Foulger et al. take as their focus the use of these tools by those involved in the world of education – that is, students and teachers. In particular, they focus on the use of these tools by the latter group, and ask a number of questions relating to the ways in which teachers or educators present themselves on social networking sites, of whether such presentation is appropriate for members of such a profession and also of whether educators have the right to use the tools to present themselves in a manner which differs from the ways in which they would customarily present themselves as part of the teaching profession. In effect, this raises the issue of the free-time versus work-time boundary which may be difficult to establish and maintain in the social networking world. For example, do teachers have the right to free expression online even if such expression runs contrary to the values of the institution? Conversely, do teachers have a duty to uphold the values of the educational institution in their personal online activity?

To investigate these issues, the researchers employed a research design not too dissimilar from the aforementioned study by O'Dea and Abraham, that is, data collection phases which were undertaken either side of an intervention. In the Foulger et al. study, the data collection phases consisted of students considering the ethical implications of two hypothetical scenarios involving the use of a social networking tool.

In the first data collection phase, the students were given a scenario where a teacher invites students to view his profile and accordingly the students 'add' the teacher to their own social network. During this process, however, the teacher notices what appear to be apparently illegal activities taking place on one of the students' profiles. He contacts the parents in order to inform them of this, but the parents believe the teacher has violated student privacy and complain to the administration. The second data collection phase involved the students being asked to read another scenario that was parallel to the one above, but with superficial amendments made such that it would be sufficiently different from the first so as not to appear a replication.

Between the first and second scenarios, the researchers introduced the independent variable into the study – this was a case-based reasoning intervention, developed by the researchers

Table 4.33 Cross-tabs of pre- and post-intervention decisions regarding disciplinary actions

		Post-intervention	
		Discipline	No discipline
Pre-int	Discipline	9	4
	No discipline	13	16

in order to support more informed decisions by pre-service teachers. The intervention took the form of an online homework process which was performed by the students over a two-week period between the first and second data collection stages. It included an explanation of the functionality of social networking tools, reports of specific instances where teachers had used networking sites for educational purposes, and discussions on the benefits and pitfalls of social networking in education.

After reading each of the scenarios, students were asked to reflect upon whether or not they felt that the teacher's actions warranted discipline, and to explain their reasoning for why they felt this way. These reflections were transcribed and coded using an established ethical concerns coding framework. The coding referred to whether the student had expressed a viewpoint supporting a no discipline outcome, or whether the student had expressed a view that that there should be a disciplinary outcome. These codes therefore represented two mutually exclusive response categories, and enabled the discussions of the students to be collapsed into counts of 0 or 1 (i.e. of 'no discipline' or 'discipline' categories; see Table 4.33).

Choice of test

Following the coding procedure, the researchers used the McNemar test to determine any differences in the students' reactions to the scenarios at the pre-intervention and post-intervention stages. The McNemar was chosen due to the research question examining differences at two different points in time (i.e. two conditions) with the same participants in both of these conditions, and also due to the nature of the data being analysed – the 'discipline' and 'no discipline' codlings representing a nominal level of measurement.

As a within-groups test of differences at a nominal level of measurement, the McNemar was thus the researcher's test of choice.

Results

The results of the analysis indicated that before the intervention, 31% of the students recommended discipline of the teacher in the scenario. After the intervention, the same students appeared to be taking a harder line, with 52% of students favouring a position oriented toward discipline. The pre–post difference was statistically significant, with a McNemar's test significance level of $p < 0.05$.

Students were therefore more likely to be oriented toward disciplinary action and to see a need for clearer policies to guide online conduct after reflecting on controversial cases. These results, along with several others produced by the study, led the researchers to conclude that the use of this case-based intervention as a pedagogical tool helped students become more attuned to the needs for clearer definition about the appropriate role of teachers in social networking spaces.

4.3.4 Narrative

For our very final visit to the lab of the now almost legendary reaction time/alertness study, we take as the main focus the activities of the third week, where the researcher reconfigured the set-up slightly, such that nominal data were being collected. The nominal data in question were based on the dichotomous categorization of 'yes' or 'no', relating to whether participants had completed the reaction time element of the experiment within the prescribed time limit.

Difference: between groups (the chi square test)

When one considers the mutually exclusive categories of 'yes' and 'no' alongside the 'clubbing' or 'non-clubbing' status of the participants, we can very easily see how this translates into a classic 2 × 2 grid, which would fit very nicely with a chi square analysis. Such an analysis would thus enable us to determine any significant differences between clubbers and non-clubbers in their ability to complete the exercises by the set time limit. Or, put another way, it would enable us to determine any association between clubbing activity and task completion. Typical SPSS outputs from such a test are included in Tables 4.34 and 4.35.

From Table 4.34, we can see that there does seem to be something of an association between the Thursday night outings and Friday morning completion rates, with most of the non-clubbers succeeding in completing the reaction time task within the time limit, and most of the clubbing group not succeeding at this. However, the results illustrated in Table 4.35 indicate that this association is not actually statistically significant, with a x^2 value of just 1.82 and a p value of 0.18.

Table 4.34 Cross-tabs of completion by Thursday night activities

		Friday task		
		Completed	Not completed	Total
Thursday	Clubbing	4	6	10
Activity	Non-clubbing	7	3	10
Total		11	9	20

Table 4.35 Chi square statistics of completion by Thursday night activities

	Value	df	Asymp. sig. (2-sided)	Exact sig. (2-sided)	Exact sig. (1 sided)
Pearson chi square	1.818[a]	1	.178		
Continuity correction[b]	.808	1	.369		
Likelihood ratio	1.848	1	.174		
Fisher's exact test				.370	.185
Linear-by-linear association	1.727	1	.189		
N of valid cases	20				

[a] 2 cells (50.0%) have expected count less than 5. The minimum expected count is 4. 50.
[b] Computed only for a 2 × 2 table.

(The results of the analysis could thus be expressed as $x^2 = 1.82$, df = 1, p = 0.18 [2-tailed]).

Difference: within groups (the McNemar test)

One supplemental data collection session could easily add a within-groups element to the activities of this particular Friday. If the researcher decided on this particular day to expand upon the 'Friday morning feeling' element of the study, and to incorporate something of a 'Friday afternoon recovery' perspective, then this would easily offer him the opportunity of adding a McNemar test to the ensemble of analyses being undertaken for this alertness study.

Let's say that once the categorization into 'yes' or 'no' groups had taken place (i.e. relating to those participants who had 'completed' or 'not completed' within the set time period), the experimenter decided to focus upon just those who had been out on the town during the previous night, inviting these to return to repeat their morning task performance during the afternoon. Let's say also that there are a lot more students in the 'on the town' category this time due to a *Carnage* event taking place the night before – hence the N in this case equalling a hundred participants.

Perhaps unknowingly to the students involved, the researcher is therefore now setting up a further experimental 'after lunch' condition – in other words, he is introducing an intervention which is taking place in the time between an initial and a subsequent data collection, theorizing that this particular intervention (of lunch) will have an impact on the participants' performance.

This therefore sets the scene rather nicely for a McNemar test to be brought into the equation, as we have a group of participants providing data along a nominal level of measurement (completed or not completed) in a 'before' condition, and these same group of participants providing the same nominal level data as part of an 'after' condition. The before and after in this case, of course, referring to the intervention of lunch – which is perhaps not quite as silly as it may first appear when considering the impact of nutrition on levels of alertness.

The results shown in Tables 4.36 and 4.37 show us that, although there was a difference observed between the 'before' and 'after' lunch performances, this took place in different directions.

Table 4.36 Cross-tabs of task completion before lunch by after lunch

Before	After	
	Not completed	Completed
Not completed	20	40
Completed	20	20

Table 4.37 Statistics of task completion before lunch by after lunch[a]

	Before and After
N	100
Chi square[b]	6.017
Asymp. sig.	.014

[a] McNemar Test.
[b] Continuity corrected.

Twenty participants who completed in the morning failed to do so in the afternoon, while forty participants failed to complete in the morning but did so in the afternoon. This suggests that lunch between the two testing periods was having an impact on the participants' task completing ability (to its improvement more than its detriment), reflected by the p value of 0.014.

(The results of the analysis could thus be expressed as McNemar $x^2 = 6.02$, N = 100, p = 0.014 [2-tailed]).

4.3.5 Further reading

Field, A. P. (2005). *Discovering Statistics using SPSS (and Sex, Drugs and Rock 'n' Roll)* 2nd Edition. Sage. section 16.2.

Brace, N., Kemp, R. and Snelgar, R. (2009). *SPSS for Psychologists* 4th Edition. Palgrave Macmillan. chapter 3, sections 1, 2 and 3 and chapter 4, sections 1, 2 and 3.

Howitt, D. and Cramer, D. (2008). *Introduction to SPSS in Psychology* 4th Edition. Pearson Prentice Hall. shapter 13.

Howitt, D. and Cramer, D. (2008). *Introduction to Statistics in Psychology 4th Edition*. Pearson Prentice Hall. chapter 14.

4.4 Summary

This final chapter has attempted to move, as smoothly as possible, from the descriptive approaches of summarizing data toward the inferential approaches of establishing relationships between variables and generalizing from samples to populations – the area probably considered as the most challenging by first year psychology students

In order to reduce the 'challenge' as much as possible, the chapter has adopted a highly structured approach that reflects the areas included within the chapters encountered thus far, that is, of describing inferential statistics from the perspectives of (1) levels of measurement, (2) research design, and (3) the research question itself – of whether we are attempting to uncover differences or similarities.

Using these three perspectives, it has firstly described the techniques to be considered when analysing scale data as part of parametric procedures (i.e. the Pearson correlation coefficient when investigating association, and the dependent and independent t-tests when testing for, respectively, within-group and between-group differences). It has then proceeded to consider non-parametric approaches used with data of an ordinal level of measurement (i.e. the Spearman correlation coefficient when investigating association, and the Wilcoxon and Mann-Whitney tests when testing for within-group and between-group differences), before finally focusing on non-parametric tests for nominal level data (i.e. the chi square and the McNemar for the respective between and within-group variants).

Throughout the chapter, and for each of the eight aforementioned analytical techniques, analogies have been drawn and examples offered as appropriate just as with preceding chapters – but much use has also been made in this final section of SPSS outputs as a method of providing the typical outputs which you, as psychology students, will most probably be generating and interpreting.

1. The non-parametric equivalent of the paired t-test is the:
   a. Mann-Whitney U test.
   b. Wilcoxon signed ranks test.
   c. Friedman test.
   d. Kruskall-Wallis test.

2. An independent t-test is used to test for:
   a. Differences between means of groups containing different people when the data are normally distributed, have equal variances and data are at least interval.
   b. Differences between means of groups containing different people when the data are not normally distributed or have unequal variances.
   c. Differences between means of groups containing the same people when the data are normally distributed, have equal variances and data are at least interval.
   d. Differences between means of groups containing the same people when the data are not normally distributed or have unequal variances.

3. Which of the following are assumptions underlying the use of the independent t-test?
   a. The data should be normally distributed.
   b. The samples being tested should have approximately equal variances.
   c. The data should be collected at a scale level of measurement.
   d. All of the above.

4. The non-parametric equivalent of the two-sample independent t-test is the:
   a. Mann-Whitney U test.
   b. Wilcoxon signed ranks test.

   c. Friedman test.

   d. Kruskall-Wallis test.

5. Which is an assumption of chi-square?

   a. That the data are normally distributed.

   b. That each participant contributes data to only one cell.

   c. That the data is continuous.

   d. That there is little variability amongst the data.

6. Twenty people took part in a study in which they completed two questionnaires: one that measured musical ability and one that measured their mathematical aptitude. The two sets of scores were then analysed to determine if the two skills were related. Which research design was used in the study?

   a. An observational study.

   b. A case study.

   c. A correlational study.

   d. An experiment.

7. The within-participants equivalent of the Mann-Whitney test is the:

   a. Chi square test.

   b. Wilcoxon signed ranks test.

   c. Independent t-test.

   d. One-way Anova.

8. What is the name of the test that is used to assess the relationship between two ordinal variables?

   a. Spearman's rho.

   b. Phi.

   c. Cramer's phi coefficient.

   d. Chi square.

9. A positive correlation shows that:

   a. Two variables are unrelated.

   b. As one score increases so does the other.

   c. As one score increases so the other decreases.

   d. Both a and b.

10. A dependent t-test is used to test for:

   a. Differences between means of groups containing different people when the data are normally distributed, have equal variances and data are at least interval.
   b. Differences between means of groups containing different people when the data are not normally distributed or have unequal variances.
   c. Differences between means of groups containing the same people when the data are normally distributed, have equal variances and data are at least interval.
   d. Differences between means of groups containing same people when the data are not normally distributed or have unequal variances.

And finally ...

Well, that about wraps it up for this book. As was said at the start, this was in no way meant to be a comprehensive account of the world of statistical analysis as there are plenty of other books around which cover the whole spectrum. (If we think of the 'sage on the stage' or the 'guide on the side' analogy, this book is definitely a case of the latter!) Hopefully though, the use of examples, scenarios and synopses of quantitative studies from the literature has helped to portray statistics as a useful tool for psychologists – and the avoidance of numbers (wherever possible) will have helped put across the idea that data analysis in psychology is still fundamentally concerned with people rather than calculations. It might be helpful though, to reflect on what we've covered in order to reinforce these ideas of 'stats is just a tool' and 'it's still about people' ...

To help get the message across, the book adopted what will hopefully have been a reasonably user-friendly structure, and one perhaps even relatively easy to memorize and utilize when dealing with statistics. Starting off way back in Chapter 1 with the (very) basics of analysis – the notions of research design, variables and their levels of measurement – it described how we can best conceptualize these basics in order to make the most appropriate choices for our initial analyses – i.e. the descriptive or exploratory statistics described in Chapter 2.

This second chapter then put the Chapter 1 concepts to work by showing how they need to be matched to the appropriate measures of central tendency and dispersion (so that we would never use the mean to summarize nominal data, for example), and then went further by demonstrating how it is not just important to determine typical scores and spreads of scores, but also to be aware of how a given score relates to all others – cue Z-scores and percentiles!

Following the Chapter 2 treatment of descriptive statistics, we took a step back and thought a little more about our data before steaming ahead too quickly into the zone of inferential analysis. Chapter 3 was therefore something of a reflective chapter, serving to 'bridge' the two major analytical approaches of descriptive and inferential statistics by outlining the considerations or data checks that we should make before going ahead with parametric or non-parametric analyses. These included an understanding of the relationship between samples and populations (with reference to standard error), appreciating the importance of explicit hypotheses (and of the concepts of probability and statistical significance which enable us to reject the null) and of course being aware of the requirements or 'assumptions' which must be met for parametric tests to be used.

By the time of the final chapter then, we should have found ourselves in a sufficiently informed position to be able to run those inferential tests (Chi, McNemar, Pearson, Spearman, Mann-Whitney, Wilcoxon and of course the independent and related t), and also to be able to select each on the basis of our knowledge of design, measurement and the nature of research questions themselves, all as acquired via Chapters 1 to 3.

So if you've made it this far, and without skipping too many bits, then you should feel a bit more at home with all this stuff than when you first looked at the front cover. It won't have made you a stats genius as that was never its aim (and there are plenty of other texts out there for that, if that indeed is what you want) but it should hopefully have succeeded in its real aim: of helping, just a bit, to reduce that 'OMG!' reaction which so often occurs after the very first lecture on any research methods module....

Good luck :–).

Appendix: Data used in Chapter 4

This short appendix includes some of the data which were used to generate a number of the sample outputs included in the chapter on inferential statistics. Not all the data used in that chapter are included here, as after all the theme of the book is based on verbal explanations rather than numerical calculations. Rather, it includes just one set of data corresponding to each one of the eight tests covered in this book (just in case you'd like some practice at SPSS input as well as interpreting SPSS output).

Independent t-test

Clubbing	240	400	360	440	320	200	240	200	180	340
Non-clubbing	240	320	220	160	120	180	160	140	280	220

Paired t-test

Clubbing	240	400	360	440	320	200	240	200	180	340
Non-clubbing	240	320	220	160	120	180	160	140	280	220
Differences	0	80	140	280	200	20	80	60	−100	120

Pearson correlation coefficient

Party time (hrs)	2.25	4.00	7.25	7.75	3.75	3.75	5.00	4.50	2.50	6.00
Reaction time (ms)	240	400	360	440	320	200	240	200	180	340

Mann-Whitney test

This book	3	5	4	4	5	4	3	3	3	5
Last year's book	4	3	4	3	4	4	3	4	3	4

Wilcoxon signed ranks test

Confidence before	3	2	2	2	2	1	3	2	3	2
Confidence after	4	3	2	2	3	2	3	3	4	3

Spearman correlation coefficient

Class position	1	2	3	4	5	6	7	8	9	10	11	12	13	14	15	16	17	18	19	20
Book ratings	2	1	2	1	5	2	3	4	3	6	3	4	5	4	3	7	6	7	7	6

Chi square

	Completed	Not completed
Clubbing	4	6
Non-clubbing	7	3

McNemar test

	Not vote after	Will vote after
Not vote before	35	20
Will vote before	15	30

Glossary

Average
Generally, a term which could refer to any one of a number of measures of central tendency (mode, median, mean) but which is mostly used as an alternative term for the mean.

Bar chart
A diagram used to illustrate the frequencies in each category of a nominal variable. The length of the bar, either horizontal or vertical, being proportional to the frequency described.

Between groups
A research design oriented toward comparing different groups of participants in different conditions.

Bimodal
A distribution of scores which contains two modes (or where the distribution has two equally most frequent values).

Bivariate
Most simply, any analysis involving two variables. Most often to be found with correlational designs.

Boxplot
A diagram comprising a central box figure with a protruding whisker on each side. The limits of the whiskers indicate the minimum and maximum (and thus also range) of the distribution. The limits of the central box indicate the distance between the 25th and the 75th percentile, with the 50th percentile (or median) being marked by an interior dividing line.

Categorical variable
Another name for a nominal variable.

Causation
The instance of one variable directly affecting another. In experimental psychology, it is the independent variable which affects (or causes change to take place in) the dependent variable.

Central limit theorem
A mathematical principle that the sampling distribution of the mean will tend to form a normal curve with a sufficiently large sample size.

Central tendency
The most typical value of a set of scores, denoted via mode, median or mean.

Chi square
A test of difference, designed to establish the association between nominal variables, when those variables refer to frequencies of cases or participants. It compares the observed frequencies with the frequencies expected by chance, often within undergraduate psychology, in the form of a 2 × 2 cross tabulation.

Condition
A treatment or level of an independent variable which differs on some dimension from another treatment or level of the same independent variable. In its simplest form, an independent variable would have two conditions – (1) the experimental and (2) the control.

Confidence interval of the mean
The range of values in a sample dataset within which it is likely (i.e. that we are confident) that the population mean is to be found.

Confounding variable
Any variable or factor, other than the independent variable, which may have an (unwanted) impact on the dependent variable – and which may adversely affect the outcome of an investigation by confounding its results.

Contingency/cross-tab table
A two-dimensional diagram of the frequencies found within the categories of nominal variables.

Continuous data
Data of a scale level of measurement which are not restricted to whole numbers, and which can be expressed in fractional values.

Control

Generally, any procedure which can be used to reduce the effect of confounding variables. The term is also applied to the 'control group' in an experimental study – that is, that which receives no treatment on the independent variable.

Correlation

A measure of the association between two or more variables.

Correlation coefficient

A numerical value indicating the size (between –1, through 0, to +1) and direction (either – or +) of the association between variables, expressed as Pearson's r (for parametric data) or Spearman's rho (for non-parametric data).

Count

An alternative term for frequency.

Dependent variable

The outcome measure of a study, that is, that which is measured by the researcher. In experimental designs, this enables one to assess the effect of manipulating the independent variable.

Descriptive stats

A set of procedures (notably those determining central tendency and dispersion) used to summarize data thus simplifying its interpretation.

Dichotomous

A measurement on which there can be only two responses, for example, Yes/No.

Difference score

The difference between a participant's or group's scores on a test taken at two points in time, usually within a before and after scenario.

Dispersion

The extent to which scores vary around a central value.

Distribution-free tests

Tests which make no assumptions regarding the form of the population distribution. An alternative term for non-parametric tests.

Effect
The influence of one variable on another, most commonly used regarding the influence of the independent on the dependent variable.

Experiment
A research design in which an investigator manipulates an independent variable to measure its effects on a dependent variable while controlling for all other factors. Assuming random allocation into conditions has been achieved, the results can be used to establish a cause and effect relationship.

Experimental group
The group which receives a treatment in an experiment which differs from that received by the control group. The treatment reflecting the condition, or level of the independent variable, under study.

Experimental hypothesis
A prediction that there will be significant relationship between two variables, or that the manipulation of an independent variable will have a significant effect on a dependent variable.

Frequency
The extent to which cases are to be found within particular categories.

Independent variable
The variable manipulated by the researcher in order to determine its effect upon the dependent variable.

Inferential statistics
The branch of statistics by which we can generalize beyond observations of samples to inferences about populations, based on the testing of hypotheses or predictions.

Independent t-test
A test comparing the means of two different groups of participants when parametric assumptions have been met.

Interquartile range
The range of the central 50% of all scores or observations within a dataset.

Kurtosis
A measure of the pointedness or flatness of a given distribution curve.

Levene
A test to determine whether the variances of two independent groups can be considered equal.

Likert
A rating (ordinal) scale designed to elicit the extent to which participants agree with a series of statements for example, ranging from strongly agree to strongly disagree.

Mann-Whitney U
The non-parametric equivalent to the independent t-test, used to determine significant differences in ranks between two independent groups.

McNemar
A non-parametric test used to determine significant differences in response frequencies (i.e. at the nominal level) within a group of participants, usually via a before and after testing design.

Mean
The preferred measure of central tendency used with scale data, calculated by summing all scores and then dividing the result by the number in the sample.

Median
The score which occupies the central position of any given dataset when all scores have been placed in order.

Mode
The most frequent score of a given dataset, most often used as the measure of central tendency for data of a nominal level of measurement.

Non-parametric
Relating to tests of data which make no assumptions concerning population parameters. Also known as distribution-free tests.

Normal distribution
A symmetrical bell-shaped curve which is produced when the majority of scores cluster around the central value of the scores with fewer scores being found as the distance from the central value is increased.

Null hypothesis
A prediction that there will be no significant relationship between two variables, or that there will be no significant effect on a dependent variable by manipulating an independent variable.

Ordinal

A scale of measurement in which scores can be placed in order of magnitude, but where the distance between the points on the scale cannot be assumed to be equal.

Outlier

A extreme score or observation which can have a distorting effect when producing summary statistics such as the mean or range.

Paired t-test

A test comparing the means of the same group of participants, usually taken at different points in time, when parametric assumptions have been met.

Parametric

Relating to tests of data which make assumptions concerning population parameters, that is, that scores represent a scale level, that they are normally distributed, and in the case of between-groups design, that the variances of the scores of each group are approximately equal.

Percentile

A measure indicating a score's position in relation to other scores, via the proportion of scores below that particular value.

Qualitative research

The branch of research less concerned with numerical data, and which seeks to probe more deeply, via techniques such as discourse analysis, to enable greater understanding than would be possible by statistical analysis alone.

Quantitative research

The branch of research concerned with measuring the magnitude of a phenomenon, or of counting its instances; this emphasis on numerical data thus allowing statistical techniques to be used in its analysis.

Quartile

The three scores within a dataset which separate the entire dataset into four equal parts, positioned at the 25th, 50th and 75th percentile positions.

Range

The difference between the maximum and minimum values of a dataset, representing the simplest measure of dispersion.

Related design
An alternative term for the within-groups design.

Sample
The participants taking part in a research study (or their scores), aimed to represent those of the population from which they are drawn.

Sampling distribution of the mean
The probability distribution of means for random samples drawn from a population.

Sampling error
The extent to which samples will vary from the population from which they were drawn.

Statistically significant
An outcome of hypotheses testing in which the null hypothesis is rejected.

Skew
A non-symmetrical distribution of scores, where many cases fall at one end of a distribution, and few at the other.

Standard deviation
The average amount by which scores in a dataset deviate from the mean score.

Standard error of the mean
The standard deviation of a distribution of means – a measure of the average amount by which sample means deviate from the population mean.

Standard score
An alternative term for the Z-score.

Statistic
Any measurement of participants within a sample can be described as a statistic, contrasted with that of the parameters of a population.

Type I error
The act of rejecting the null hypothesis when it is true (i.e. of obtaining a statistically significant result when there is actually no significant effect taking place).

Type II error

Failing to reject the null hypothesis when it is false (i.e. of obtaining a non-significant result when there is actually a significant effect taking place).

Variable

Factors or characteristics which can have different values (i.e. vary) and which can be measured.

Variance

A measure of dispersion, based on the average squared deviation of scores around a mean.

Within groups

A research design oriented toward comparing the same groups of participants in different conditions, usually being measured at different points in time.

Z-score

A value indicating the distance of any score from the mean score of a dataset, as measured by the number of standard deviations that particular score is from the mean.

References

Ajzen, I. (1991). The Theory of Planned Behavior. *Organizational Behavior and Human Decision Processes*, 50, 179–211.

Alexander, C. M. and Hines, M. (2002). Sex Differences in Response to Children's Toys in Nonhuman Primates. *Evolution and Human Behaviour*, 23, 467–79.

Aron, A., Norman, C. C., Aron, E. N., McKenna, C. and Heyman, R. E. (2000). Couples' Shared Participation in Novel and Arousing Activities and Experienced Relationship Quality. *Journal of Personality and Social Psychology*, 78, 273–84.

Babbie, E. (2006). *The Practice of Social Research* 10th edition. Wadsworth, Thomson Learning.

Bandura, A., Ross, D. and Ross, S. A. (1961). Transmission of Aggression through Imitation of Aggressive Models. *Journal of Abnormal and Social Psychology*, 63, 573–82.

BBC News (2 Nov. 2009). *Obese 'struggle to earn living'*. http://news.bbc.co.uk/1/hi/health/8337512.stm [accessed 10th December 2009].

Biddle, S. J. H. and Wang, C. K. J. (2003). Motivation and Self-Perception Profiles and Links with Physical Activity in Adolescent Girls. *Journal of Adolescence*, 26, 687–701.

Brace, N., Kemp, R. and Snelgar, R. (2009). *SPSS for Psychologists 4th Edition*. Palgrave Macmillan.

Breakwell, G. M., Hammond, S., Fife-Schaw, C. and Smoth, J. A. (2006). *Research Methods in Psychology 3rd Edition*. London: Sage.

Brebner, J. (2003). Gender and Emotions. *Personality and Individual Differences*, 34, 387–94.

Bressler, E. R. and Balshine, S. (2004). The Influence of Humor on Desirability, *Evolution and Human Behavior*, 27, 29–39.

Bressler, E. R., Martin, R. A. and Balshine, S. (2006). Production and Appreciation of Humor as Sexually Selected Traits. *Evolution and Human Behavior*, 27, 121–30.

Buckley, W. (2007). Ali? Laver? Best? No, the Williams sisters. *The Observer*, 16 September 2007.

Burkeman, O. (2006). How Many Hits? *The Guardian*, 11 November 2006.

Buss, D. M. and Schmitt, D. P. (1993). Sexual Strategies Theory: an Evolutionary Perspective on Human Mating. *Psychological Review*, 100, 204–32.

Cassady, J. C. (2004). The Influence of Cognitive Test Anxiety across the Learning–Testing Cycle. *Learning and Instruction*, 14, 569–92.

Conway, M. and Bannister, P. (2007). High Quality Science A Level. *The Psychologist*, Volume 20, 10th Edition, October 2007, 608–9.

Coolican, H. (2009). *Research Methods and Statistics in Psychology*. London: Hodder & Stoughton.

Darley, J. M. and Latane, B. (1968). Bystander Intervention in Emergencies: Diffusion of Responsibility. *Journal of Personality and Social Psychology*, 8, 377–83.

Dean, L. M., Willis, F. N. and Hewitt, J. (1975). Initial Interaction Distance among Individuals Equal and an Equal in Military Rank. *Journal of Personality and Social Psychology*, 32, 294–9.

Deary, I. J., Thorpe, G., Wilson, V., Starr, J. M. and Whalley, L. J. (2003) Population Sex Differences in IQ at Age 11: the Scottish Mental Survey 1932. *Intelligence*, 31, 533–52.

Donders, F. C. (1868). On the Speed of Mental Processes. Translated by W. G. Koster (1969), *Acta Psychologica*, 30, 412–31.

Festinger, L. and Carlsmith, J. M. (1959). Cognitive Consequences of Forced Compliance. *Journal of Abnormal and Social Psychology*, 58, 203–10.

Field, A. P. (2005). *Discovering Statistics Using SPSS 2nd Edition*. London: Sage.

Foulger, T. S., Ewbank, A. D., Kay, A., Popp, S. O. and Carter, H. L. (2009). Moral Spaces in MySpace: Preservice Teachers' Perspectives about Ethical Issues in Social Networking. *Journal of Research on Technology in Education*, 42, 1–28.

Fu, M., Cheng, L., Tu, S. and Pan, W. (2007). Association between Unhealthful Eating Patterns and Unfavorable Overall School Performance in Children. *Journal of the American Dietetic Association*, 107, 1935–43.

Gardner, H. (1983). *Frames of Mind: the Theory of Multiple Intelligences*. New York: Basic Books.

Hafner, K. (2005). How Thursdays Became the New Fridays. *The New York Times*, 6 November 2005.

Holt, N. and Walker, I. (2009). *Research with People: Theory, Plans and Practicals*. Palgrave Macmillan.

Howitt, D. and Cramer, D. (2008a). *Introduction to Research Methods in Psychology 2nd Edition*. Harlow: Pearson Prentice Hall.

Howitt, D. and Cramer, D. (2008b). *Introduction to SPSS in Psychology 4th Edition*. Harlow: Pearson Prentice Hall.

Howitt, D. and Cramer, D. (2008c). *Introduction to Statistics SPSS in Psychology 4th Edition*. Harlow: Pearson Prentice Hall.

Joiner, R. J., Brosnan, M., Duffield, J., Gavin, J. and Maras, P. (2007). The Relationship between Internet Identification, Internet Anxiety and Internet Use. *Computers in Human Behavior*, 23, 1408–20.

Keegan V. (2009). Music Industry Must Change the Record. *The Guardian*, 21 May 2009.

Korat, O. (2009). The Effect of Maternal Teaching Talk on Children's Emergent Literacy as a Function of Type of Activity and Maternal Education Level. *Journal of Applied Developmental Psychology*, 30, 34–42.

Krantzer, J. H. (2007). *Statistics for the Terrified.* Pearson Education.

Lai, H., Chen, P., Chen, C., Chang, H., Peng, T. and Chang, F. (2008). Randomized Crossover Trial Studying the Effect of Music on Examination Anxiety. *Nurse Education Today*, 28, 909–16.

Lang, P. J. and Lazovik, A. D. (1963). Experimental Desensitization of a Phobia. *Journal of Abnormal and Social Psychology*, 66, 519–25.

Lazzari, M. (2009) Creative Use of Podcasting in Higher Education and Its Effect on Competitive Agency. *Computers and Education*, 52, 27–34.

Lee, C. F., Lee, J. C. and Lee, A. C. (2000). *Statistics for Business and Financial Economics 2nd Edition.* World Scientific.

Likert, R. (1932). A Technique for the Measurement of Attitudes. *Archives of Psychology*, 140, 1–55.

Lucking-Reiley, D., Bryan, D., Prasad, N. and Reeves, D. (2007). Pennies from eBay: the Determinants of Price in Online Auctions. *Journal of Industrial Economics*, 55, 223–33.

Lyn, R., Raine, A., Venables, P. H., Mednick, S. A. and Irwing, P. (2005a). Sex Differences on the WISC-R in Mauritius. *Intelligence*, 33, 527–33.

Lyn, R., Raine, A., Venables, P. H., Mednick, S. A. and Irwing, P. (2005b). Sex Differences in 3 Year Olds on the Boehm Test of Basic Concepts: Some Data from Mauritius. *Personality and Individual Differences*, 39, 683–8.

Maguire, E. A., Gadian, D. G., Johnsrode, J. S., Good, C. D., Ashburner, J., Frackowiack, R. S. J. and Frith, C. (2000). Navigational Related Structural Change in the Hippocampi of Taxi Drivers. *Proceedings of the National Academy of Science, USA*. 1997, 4398–403.

Matthews, C. R. (2004). Examining Problem Drinking and Eating Disorders from a Gendered Perspective in M. S. Gold. (ed) *Eating Disorders, Overeating, and Pathological Attachment to Food.* New York: Haworth Press.

McMasters, C. and Lee, C. (1991). Cognitive Dissonance in Tobacco Smokers. *Addictive Behaviors*, 6, 349–53.

McQueen, R. A. and Knusses, C. (2006). *Introduction to Research Methods and Statistics.* Hants: Pearson Prentice Hall.

McVeigh, T. (2001). Race Split in Britain Exposed by Survey. *The Observer*, 25 November 2001.

Miles, J. (2001). *Research Methods & Statistics.* Exeter: Crucial Pubs.

Miles, J. and Banyard, P. (2007). *Understanding and Using Statistics in Psychology.* London: Sage.

Milgram, S. and Toch, H. (1969). Collective Behavior: Crowds and Social Movements in G. Lindzey and E. Aronson (eds) *The Handbook of Social Psychology*, 4, 507–610. Reading, MA: Addison Wesley.

Miller, L. C. and Fishkin, S. A. (1997). On the Dynamics of Human Bonding and Reproductive Success in J. Simpson and D. T. Kenrick (eds) *Evolutionary Social Psychology*. Hillsdale, NJ: Erlbaum.

Morrison, N. (2009). Remote Control. *The Times Educational Supplement*, 6 November, 2009.

Noyes, J. and Garland, K. (2005). Students' Attitudes toward Books and Computers. *Computers in Human Behavior*, 21, 233–41.

O'Dea, J. A. and Abraham, S. (2000). Improving the Body Image, Eating Attitudes and Behaviors of Young Male and Female Adolescents: a New Educational Approach That Focuses on Self-Esteem. *International Journal of Eating Disorders*, 28, 43–57.

Patten, C. J. D., Kircher, A., Östlund, J. and Nilsson, L. (2004). Using Mobile Telephones: Cognitive Workload and Attention Resource Allocation. *Accident Analysis & Prevention*, 36, 341–50.

Pedersen, W. C., Miller, L. C., Putcha-Bhagavatula, A. D. and Yang, Y. (2002). Evolved Sex Differences in the Number of Partners Desired? The Long and the Short of It. *Psychological Science*, 13, 157–61.

Piliavin, I. M., Rodin, J. A. and Piliavin, P. (1969). Good Samaritanism: an Underground Phenomenon? *Journal of Personality and Social Psychology*, 13, 289–99.

PoliticsHome (2009). *Parliament's Reputation Returns to Pre-Expenses Level*. PoliticsHome. http://page.politicshome.com/uk/parliaments_reputation_returns_to_pre_expenses_level.html [accessed 10 December 2009].

Pollard, M. (2007). *Internet Access 2007*. Office for National Statistics. http://www.statistics.gov.uk/pdfdis/inta0807.pdf [accessed 10 December 2009].

Pollitt, E. (1995). Does Breakfast Make a Difference in School? *Journal of the American Dietetic Association*, 95, 1134–9.

Pryor, F. (2007). Have Radiohead Marked Music's Future? *BBC News*, 10 October 2007. http://news.bbc.co.uk/1/hi/entertainment/7026601.stm [accessed 19 December 2009].

Rammstedt, B. and Rammsayer, T. H. (2000). Sex Differences in Self-Estimates of Different Aspects of Intelligence. *Personality and Individual Differences*, 29, 869–80.

Schachter, S. (1959). *The Psychology of Affiliation*. Stanford: Stanford University Press.

Seaton, M. (2006). Pedalling Fictions. *The Guardian*, 30 June 2006.

Shapiro, C. M., Auch, C., Reimer, M., Kayumov, M., Heslegrave, R., Huterera, N., Driver, H. and Devins, G. M. (2006). A New Approach to the Construct of Alertness . *Journal of Psychosomatic Research*, 60, 595–603.

Sherwin, A. (2007). How Much Is Radiohead's Online Album Worth? Nothing at All, Say a Third of Fans. *The Times*, 11 October 2007.

Sheskin, D. J. (2003). *Handbook of Parametric and Nonparametric Statistical Procedures*. Chapman and Hall.

Shiels, M. (2008). Facebook Imposes Site Facelift. *BBC News*, 11 September 2008. http://news.bbc.co.uk/1/hi/technology/7609555.stm [accessed 10th December 2009].

Smithers, R. (2005). Students Happier with Traditional Academic Courses. *The Guardian*, 8 September 2005.

Sprafkin, J. N., Liebert, R. M. and Poulos, R. W. (1975). Effects of a Pro-Social Televised Example on Children's Helping. *Journal of Experimental Child Psychology*, 20, 119–26.

Stuart, K. (2009). Is Marketing More Important Than Game Quality? *The Guardian*, 17 November 2009.

Thurstone, L. L. (1938). *Primary Mental Abilities*. Chicago: University of Chicago Press.

Topping, A. (2009). Collapse in Illegal Sharing and Boom in Streaming Brings Music to Executives' Ears. *The Guardian*, 12 July 2009.

Trivers, R. L. (1972). Parental Investment and Sexual Selection in B. Campbell (ed.) *Sexual Selection and the Descent of Man*. Chicago: Aldine.

Tsang, M. M., Ho, S. and Liang, T. (2004). Consumer Attitudes Toward Mobile Advertising:An Empirical Study. *International Journal of Electronic Commerce*, 8, 65–78.

Vuorela, M. and Nummenmaa, L. (2004). How Undergraduate Students Meet a New Learning Environment? *Computers in Human Behavior*, 20, 763–77.

Watts, K. P. (1953). Influences Affecting the Results of a Test of High Grade Intelligence. *British Journal of Psychology*, 44, 359–67.

Wimmer, R. D. and Dominick, J. R. (1987) *Mass Media Research: An Introduction*. Wadsworth.

Windle, M. (2004). Retrospective Use of Alcohol and Other Substances by College Students: Psychometric Properties of a New Measure. *Addictive Behaviors*, 30, 337–42.

Witte, R. S. and Witte, J. S. (2004). *Statistics 7th Edition*. Wiley.

Young, R. M., Hasking, P. A., Oeic, T. P. S. and Loveday, W. (2007). Validation of the Drinking Refusal Self-Efficacy Questionnaire— Revised in an Adolescent Sample (DRSEQ-RA). *Addictive Behaviors*, 32, 862–68.

Answers to self-tests

1. Ordinal level data are characterized by:
   Data that can be meaningfully arranged by order of magnitude.

2. A Repeated measures design would be appropriate for which of the following situations?
   A researcher would like to study the effect of alcohol on reaction time.

3. Which of the following is a between groups design?
   Different participants perform in each condition.

4. What is the dependent variable in experimental research?
   The variable which is measured, to see results of an experiment.

5. Temperature measured along the Fahrenheit scale can be considered as:
   Scale data.

6. Participants take a simulated driving test twice, in one condition they have no alcohol, in the other they have enough alcohol to take them over the legal limit. Is this design:
   Repeated measures.

7. An experimental design in which all subjects participate in all experimental conditions is known as:
   A Repeated measures design.

8. If a researcher wanted to investigate the effect of cigarette smoking by mothers on birth defects in children she would most likely conduct:
   A correlational study.

9. A researcher investigates the effect of caffeine on sleeping behaviour by allocating participants into two groups, group 1 (drinking normal coffee) and group 2 (drinking decaffeinated coffee) before recording how long it takes participants to fall asleep. In this scenario:
   Time taken to sleep is the dependent variable and caffeine is the independent variable.

Chapter 2

1. What is an outlier?
   A single score that is very different form the others.
2. Which of the following is most affected by outliers?
   The mean.
3. The standard deviation is the square root of the:
   Variance.
4. Which of the following is true?
   The variance is a measure of dispersion and is the square of the standard deviation.
5. The interquartile range:
   Is usually smaller than the range.
6. Which of the following is NOT a feature of descriptive statistics?
   Descriptive statistics inform us of the nature of relationships between variables.
7. If a distribution is multi-modal, what does this mean?
   It will not be a normal distribution.
8. Which of the following is a good measure of the spread of scores?
   None of the above.
9. Which of the following is true?
   Variance is a standard formula to indicate the variability of all scores for a particular variable.
10. Dispersion is to central tendency as variance is to:
    Mean.

Chapter 3

1. Which of the following terms best describes the sentence: 'In a blind-tasting, people will not be able to tell the difference between margarine and butter'.
   A null hypothesis.
2. The assumption of homogeneity of variance is met when:
   Variances in different groups are approximately equal.
3. What is a significance level?
   A pre-set level of probability at which it will be accepted that results are due to chance or not.

4. A Type I error occurs when:
   We conclude that there is a statistically significant effect when there actually is not.

5. Another term for non-parametric tests is:
   Distribution-free tests.

6. Levene's test tests for whether:
   The variances in different groups are equal.

7. What is the conventional level of probability that is often accepted when conducting statistical tests?
   0.05.

8. A null hypothesis:
   Predicts that the experimental treatment will have no effect.

9. 'Sleep deprivation will reduce the ability to perform a complex cognitive task'. State the direction of this hypothesis:
   Directional.

Chapter 4

1. The non-parametric equivalent of the paired t-test is the:
   Wilcoxon signed ranks test.

2. An independent t-test is used to test for:
   Differences between means of groups containing different people when the data are normally distributed, have equal variances and data are at least interval.

3. Which of the following are assumptions underlying the use of the independent t-test?
   All of the above.

4. The non-parametric equivalent of the two-sample independent t-test is the:
   Mann-Whitney U test.

5. Which is an assumption of chi-square?
   That each participant contributes data to only one cell.

6. Twenty people took part in study in which they completed two questionnaires: one that measured musical ability and one that measured their mathematical aptitude. The two sets of scores were then analysed to determine if the two skills were related. Which research design was used in the study?
   A correlational study.

7. The within-participants equivalent of the Mann-Whitney test is the:
   Wilcoxon signed ranks test.

8. What is the name of the test that is used to assess the relationship between two ordinal variables?
   Spearman's rho.

9. A positive correlation shows that:
   As one score increases so does the other.

10. A dependent t-test is used to test for:
    Differences between means of groups containing the same people when the data are normally distributed, have equal variances and data are at least interval.

Index

Alpha level, 89, 90, 119, 145
Assumptions, 77, 92, 94–95, 99, 104, 110, 111, 125, 130, 132, 142–43, 156, 171, 199

Between groups design, 24, 28–29, 34, 76, 94–95, 97, 108, 110, 112, 120, 125–26, 132, 135, 137, 142, 144, 155, 156, 160–61, 165, 171–72, 177, 179, 184, 190, 194

Categorical, see /nominal level of measurement
Causation, 24, 112–13
Chi square, 109, 171–80, 182–85, 190–94
Confounding variable, 2, 17–18, 35
Continuous, 18–21, 29, 32–33, 35, 60, 62, 70, 100
Control variable, 2, 17, 35
Correlation coefficient, 32, 109, 111–12, 118–19, 130–32, 139–43, 147–49, 159–65, 168–71, 183, 194

Dependent variable, 1, 2, 4, 15–18, 21, 24, 29, 30, 32–35, 41, 48, 50, 62, 69, 73, 103, 111, 113, 115–16, 122, 123, 125–26, 129, 132, 156, 158, 175
Dichotomous, 103, 183, 186, 190
Directional, 85, 88, 89, 100
Discrete, 3–9, 11, 13, 16, 18, 20–21, 28–29, 32–33, 35, 60, 70

Dispersion, 40, 51–63, 67, 72, 83–85, 116, 118, 119, 198

Experimental Hypothesis, 85–91

Factor, see Independent variable

Homogeneity of variance, 99

Independent design, see Between Groups design
Independent variable, 1, 2, 4, 15–18, 21–25, 27–35, 48, 50, 92, 94, 103, 111, 113, 122, 129, 130, 132, 139, 156, 158, 178, 188
Interquartile range, 52, 60, 64, 72
Interval level of measurement, 4, 7, 22

Kurtosis, 93–95, 97, 99, 101–102, 113–19, 136–39

Levene, 94, 95, 97–98, 101–102, 113–14, 136–37
Likert, 11, 13, 15, 151–53, 160, 162, 164, 171, 180

Mann-Whitney, 109, 142–45, 154–55, 157, 159–61, 165–67, 180, 194, 199
McNemar, 109, 171–72, 175–77, 185–87, 189–94, 199
Mean, 21, 26, 40–50, 53–55, 57–58, 60, 63, 65–66, 71–73,

Mean – *continued*
    79–84, 87, 92–95, 97,
    100–101, 112–17, 135–38,
    145–47, 159, 165–68, 198
Median, 40–45, 47–50, 60,
    63, 72, 100, 168
Mode, 40–48, 50, 55, 56,
    60, 72, 100

Nominal level of measurement,
    3–11, 13, 16, 18, 20, 21, 29,
    33–35, 41, 47, 50, 60, 72,
    92, 100–101, 108–109, 141,
    171–94
Normal distribution, 46, 60, 80,
    83, 92–95, 97, 104, 111–15,
    117–19, 121, 125, 130, 135,
    137–39, 142–44, 164, 171,
    184, 186
Null hypothesis, 85–91, 104,
    176–77, 199

Ordinal level of measurement,
    3–8, 11–13, 15–16, 18, 20–21,
    28–29, 33, 35, 41, 44, 50, 60,
    67, 70, 72, 76, 92, 100–101,
    108–109, 141, 170, 180, 194

Paired design, *see* Within Groups
    design
Pearson Correlation Coefficient,
    32, 109, 111–12, 117–19,
    130–34, 139–40, 142–43, 148,
    161–65, 169, 174, 183, 194, 199
Percentage, 1, 14, 63–64, 185
Percentile, 40, 42, 62–73, 198
Predictor variable, 111

Random, 26, 48
Range, 39–40, 52–56, 60, 67, 72,
    100, 186
Rank, 19–20, 42, 62, 67, 143–48,
    165–69, 171
Ratio level of measurement, 14,
    22, 86, 88
Related design, *see* Within Groups
    design

Repeated measures design, *see*
    Within Groups design

Sampling distribution, 80, 83
Scale level of measurement, 3–8,
    13–14, 16, 18–19, 21–22,
    29, 33–35, 41–42, 44, 50,
    54, 60, 67–68, 70, 72–73,
    76, 92–95, 97–98, 100,
    104, 108–41
Significant, 2, 10, 19, 25–26, 29,
    31–32, 39, 49, 57–58, 85–91,
    97–103
Skew, 46, 93–102, 113–19, 122,
    135–39, 160, 164
Spearman Correlation
    Coefficient, 109, 142–43,
    147–49, 159–64, 168–70, 183,
    194, 199
Standard deviation, 26, 40,
    53–60, 63, 65–66, 72–73, 80,
    83, 91, 116
Standard error of the mean,
    78–84, 94, 97, 101, 103, 113,
    117, 135, 138–39, 199

t-test, independent, 26, 95, 99,
    109–14, 117, 120–21, 123,
    125, 131, 135–37, 194
t-test, paired, 109, 110–11, 115–17,
    125–26, 128–30, 137–38, 143
Type I & II errors, 90–91

Unrelated design, *see* Between
    Groups design

Wilcoxon, 109, 142–47, 150–55,
    161, 165–67, 180, 194, 199
Within groups design, 23,
    25–27, 29–30, 33–35,
    50, 60, 76, 100, 108–11,
    115–16, 137 143, 146,
    150, 151, 155, 166, 171,
    172, 175–76, 185–86, 190,
    192, 194

Z score, 40, 62–73, 198